PREACH E.A.S.Y.

A Practical Guide to Preaching That Effectively and Authentically Shares Your Story

by
Gamal T. Alexander

PREACH EASY: Preaching that Effectively and Autentically Shares Your Story

Published by Watersprings Publishing, a division of
Watersprings Media House, LLC.

P.O. Box 1284
Olive Branch, MS 38654

www.waterspringsmedia.com

Contact publisher for bulk orders and permission requests.

Copyrights © 2019 by Gamal Alexander

All rights reserved. No part of this publication may be reproduced, distributed, or transmitted in any form or by any means, including photocopying, recording, or other electronic or mechanical methods, without the prior written permission of the publisher, except in the case of brief quotations embodied in critical reviews and certain other noncommercial uses permitted by copyright law.

Printed in the United States of America.

Library of Congress Control Number: 2019917683

ISBN-13: 978-1-948877-40-4

TABLE OF CONTENTS

	Acknowledgments	1
	Introduction	3
Chapter One	It's E.A.S.Y.	6
Chapter Two	The Process	16
Chapter Three	So It Begins!	24
Chapter Four	Treasure Hunting	36
Chapter Five	When a Plan Comes Together	49
Chapter Six	His Story, Your Story	68
	Selected Bibliography	77
	Additional Resources	78
	Preach E.A.S.Y. Worksheet	80
	About The Author	84

ACCLAIM FOR PREACH E.A.S.Y

"Preach E.A.S.Y. is an insightful look at homiletics that will be an asset to anyone called upon to share the gospel. Regardless of your training or previous experience, if you have to preach and want to make the preparation process simpler and easier, Preach E.A.S.Y. is the book for you." - *Dr. Kimberly Credit, Preaching Professor and Senior Pastor Mt Zion Baptist Church, NJ.*

"As a leader who trains other leaders, I've found the Preach E.A.S.Y. system almost to good to limit to those who preach. This will be a valuable resource that helps all of us who tell the story of Jesus for years to come." - *Dr. MyRon Edmonds, Grace Community Church. Cleveland, OH*

"For years, the cumbersome journey from scripture to sermon has been made more difficult for lack of a simple and repeatable homiletical process. Preach E.A.S.Y. offers a practical and straight-forward approach to the text that gives room for the preacher to arrive at the essence of the message without undo hardship. Preachers on every level of the craft would be benefitted by following the approach shared in this book."
- *Pastor Lola Johnston, Senior Pastor Woodbridge SDA Church, Woodbridge, VA*

"Finally! This is a book that so many of us have been looking for and desperately needed. Gamal shares a simple method to take the stress out of preaching while helping us make the good news even clearer to our hearers. I have been blessed to be coached in the Preach E.A.S.Y. method and it blessed my preaching ministry tremendously. I am so glad that it is now available in this simple, easy to read, and practical book. Read this book and watch your sermon process become simpler and messages become clearer." - *Kymone Hinds, CEO "Ideas to Life"*

"I wish this book was written 20 years ago, when I started pastoral ministry. Gamal has found a way to make the hard work of preparation simple without removing the necessary rigor it takes to create a sermon. This book belongs in every preacher's library!" - *Dr. C. Wesley Knight. Preaching Professor, Senior Pastor, ReVision Church, Atlanta, GA*

ACKNOWLEDGMENTS

I have been blessed with an amazing tribe that works tirelessly to bring out the best in me. I consider them my family. Precious people who won't allow me to wallow in the sinking sand of the mediocre but walk alongside me as I continue to learn and grow. Honestly, there isn't anything that I could say to these people that would repay them for the time, energy, and care that they have put into this project and into me. I really can't thank my family enough. But that doesn't mean that I cannot try…

Thank you.

One of my closest friends saw this project long before I did and encouraged me. You know who you are. My friend, my brother, I consider you family. I thank you.

Some of my most cherished friends witnessed this book as it was being birthed and invested much of their time, energy, and expertise to help me bring it to pass. They read, edited, listened to my ideas, offered feedback and suggestions, and did everything within their power to make this project something of which we could all be proud. These special people treated this project like it was their own. They belong to me as well. They are my adopted family. To them I say, "Thank you".

To those who have supported my endeavors and have journeyed with me as I have followed my dreams, I cannot leave you out. Isn't it amazing how people you have little history with can come to mean so much to you? You mean so much to me. You are also family. Thank you.

To the family bound to me by blood, know that I wouldn't trade you for anything… or anyone. My parents, siblings, aunts, uncles, cousins, (and two of the most precious daughters a guy could ever have) deserve words of appreciation much more poetic than these. Maybe they'll come to me one day. You supported me, you prayed for me, you encouraged me, and you celebrated me. I love you too. To my biological family I say "Thank you".

To the reader of this book, I now consider you a part of my family as well. I'm looking forward to taking this journey with you and I thank you for the privilege of allowing this book to be your guide.

I appreciate my entire family. More than you will ever know.

INTRODUCTION

Conventional wisdom says, "Be bad first, then get better". That makes sense to me. After all, the journey of a thousand miles does begin with the first step, and for most of us that first step is guaranteed to be shaky at best. Personally, I don't have a problem with creativity and shaky first steps, it's not starting off bad that's my problem. My problem is going from bad to mediocre and staying there because I'm constantly overwhelmed with the overall creative process. When it comes to preaching, I want to give God my best. I'm sure you do too. Yet there's something about crafting something creative week after week that often gets the best of me.

Many of us do have a similar problem. Why? Because I think creativity, for the most part, is misunderstood.

Often, when we think about creativity and those who are good at it, what comes to mind is the image of the painter who sits meditatively before a blank canvas guided by nothing more than genius and imagination. Every brushstroke brings to life a purely original masterpiece that effortlessly burst onto the canvas. Taking its place in the world.

Or maybe we think of the musicians who spend days on end in the studio driven by a desire to unleash the creative floodgates that have been pent up inside. After hours of agonizing attempts, the song finally emerges as a beautiful melody takes its place among the classics.

Maybe you can identify with the author engaged in battle with the demon of writer's block who stubbornly slaves away at the computer birthing the manuscript one word at a time, until all of a sudden, the floodgates open and the project is free at last! This is how we see creativity. This is what we think will work.

And it DOES work. We hear the stories. We witness the testimonies. We have all seen the results. We have all borne witness to the greats in every arena, including ours, operating in the ionosphere of their ingenuity. We have seen the great preachers in action. We have sat in the pews as they have blown our minds. We admire their work even as it reminds us that we have a long way to go. And we want to get there! We strive to be the kinds of preachers that effectively deliver God's Word no matter where the assignment takes us. We want to be effective communicators regardless of the circumstance. So, we struggle, and we strive. We work harder. We study more. We attend another seminar. We take another class. We worry and we pray.

But what if there was another way? Allow me to offer a different perspective:

The secrets that make the great preachers great and the consistent preachers consistent aren't really secrets at all. Rather, they are a way of looking at creativity that we most often ignore. Conventional wisdom says that we are at our most creative when we start from scratch. We are told that it is beginning with the blank slate that earns us the right to truly feel as if we are making a meaningful contribution to the world. The problem with this idea is that it doesn't let you see behind the scenes. The most creative performers have teams that edit and produce and help to shape and mold the final product. The most effective artists are given the benefit of time to listen to, or look at their work again and again until they see the flaws in their work and eliminate as many as possible. They have teams. They have time. You, my friend, have an upcoming appointment with a waiting congregation. The rules are different for you.

The rules are different, but the mission is not impossible. Research shows that the most creative among us do not start from scratch at all. Rather, in the absence of a team and adequate time, they have a technique! If they have one, why can't you? What if you had a preparation process and a consistent structure you could rely on to get you started every week? What if you didn't have to race against the clock because you were wondering, "What am I going to say?", "How am I going to say it?" and "Will this actually work?" The most creative among us have a formula for their creativity that they can rely on to help them produce again and again. Preach E.A.S.Y. is your formula. This system allows you to avoid starting from scratch, save hours of time, and instead focus on effectively, authentically sharing your story. The very next time you preach, you won't have to worry so much about finding something to say or structuring what you will say. Rather, you can dedicate yourself to polishing what you have produced using a system you can depend on. Instead of baking from scratch, Preach E.A.S.Y. delivers gourmet ingredients to your door. (Don't worry. You won't be baking this cake from a box!) You'll spend less time wondering what to cook, and more time figuring out how to make the meal that much better.

Get familiar with the book's principles. Adopt the preparation process. Master the E.A.S.Y. outline. Make this system your own. In time, I believe you will come to the same conclusion as I did. Preaching doesn't have to be intimidating. Preparation doesn't have to be hard. In fact, it can be easy.

CHAPTER ONE

IT'S E.A.S.Y.

Growing up, everything I encountered told me that great preaching had to be hard.

Maybe that's what scared me most about preaching. Maybe, deep down inside, that's what scares you. Even if I wanted to believe otherwise I just couldn't help myself. I felt my belief was justified, mostly because of what I was seeing with my own two eyes.

The year was 2004 and standing in the pulpit of the Oakwood University Campus Church in Huntsville, Alabama was one of the most gifted preachers I had ever seen, preaching one of the most amazing sermons I have ever heard. This struggling, skinny pastor serving in Gainesville, GA was being treated to a display of homiletical brilliance that would have made the great Charles Spurgeon proud. The preacher commanded the spotlight, with not much more than a Bible in his right hand and holding our collective attention in the palm of his left. The moment was Disney-level magical. We waited patiently for his every word, enjoying a ride on a roller coaster of emotions as the preacher took us on a journey from the Garden of Eden to the Garden of Gethsemane. The congregation was inspired. Me? I was in awe. If nothing else, we were all convinced that this preacher was gifted.

The preacher was indeed gifted. So gifted, in fact, that his sermon managed to leave me both inspired and discouraged at the same time. As I left the sanctuary that day, his descriptions and delivery still dancing in my head, I couldn't help but be inspired. I was first inspired by the message. He preached the gospel. Christ's victory at Calvary was celebrated and those in attendance were reminded of the victory to which they could lay claim. We all walked out of church that night feeling like we were more than conquerors. By the end of that sermon I knew that, while the enemy I fought on the "battlefields" in rural Northeast Georgia would not go quietly, and in spite of my meager resources and many rookie ministry mistakes, I was destined to make a difference. The battle I fought was a part of a war that had already been won! The "Eagle" had crushed the head of the serpent and I called to share that good news with everybody.

While the good news left me inspired, however, the same event that picked me up, let me down. The same preacher that inspired me also left me discouraged. I had been called to preach. There was no doubt in my mind about that. From childhood I had a keen awareness about what I was called to do. I KNEW I was supposed to preach. Preaching wasn't what frightened me...what scared me to death was ever being able to preach like THAT! We all claim to be allergic to mediocrity, but it was this display of gifted preaching that scared me. Gifted preachers and gifted preaching scared me back then. To be honest, sometimes they still do.

Exceptional sermons seem to flow from gifted preachers naturally. The ideas come effortlessly. The connection is second nature. The energy exudes endlessly. You and I are left speechless, amazed, bewildered and yes, discouraged. Because we've convinced ourselves that we might as well as not even try. Or at least not try too hard. No use getting our hopes up. We can't ever preach like that.

The problem with the gifted is that they always make things look easy. Sports fans know this all too well. The armchair quarterbacks criticize the best of the best mostly because of what they can do- and what we cannot. The gifted are so good at what they do that they force us to forget how difficult what they are doing actually is and how long it took for them to prepare. We just assume that LeBron James (Or Michael Jordan if you prefer) received their gifts from the basketball gods. Winners of the genetic lottery, they were blessed with abilities that us "normal" people can only hope to have. Naturally, we aren't curious about the hard work. We don't inquire about the coaching. We don't ask about the endless hours perfecting the fundamentals. We see them perform and they are excellent. They capture our imagination. They are our standards of excellence in their respective eras. Most of all, they made everything look easy.

Gifted preachers tend to do the same. With skill and sleight of hand, they make the entire experience look effortless. Like an audience watching a magician, we are impressed even if we know that there is more than meets the eye. We get so entranced by the performance that we come to the conclusion that, unless you too have these powers, there is no way that you can do what the gifted preachers do. You have to settle for the best you can do, because you could NEVER preach like that.

To make matters worse, not only are we captivated by these gifts that mystify us, but we are also overwhelmed with information on the subject of preaching that is often challenging to keep up with and sometimes difficult to understand. Every profession has its terminology, trade secrets, and sacred texts. Preaching is no different. Centuries worth of tradition and research dating back to the time of the apostles and beyond has given us lots of methodology on how to effectively communicate the message of the gospel. Research has been done. There is data in abundance. Volumes on preaching fill entire libraries covering the subject from every angle imaginable. Books of all sizes, written in various styles, from different perspectives, all tackle the same subject of "How to preach a sermon". Those who love the field of preaching can find themselves using "shop talk" without even knowing it. New books are being written every year. New journals are being published every month. New conferences are springing up every day. Who wouldn't find all of this overwhelming? How do we know which method works the best? How does the preacher know which model to follow?

When the preacher does finally select a book, attend a seminar, or otherwise decide to pursue excellence in his or her craft, they are confronted with impractical prescriptions they couldn't possibly use from day to day. Especially by people who have normal lives to live. David Buttrick's "Homiletic" is sitting on my shelf right now as an example of a classic preaching volume that is guaranteed to make your head spin and leave your eyes glossed over. (That is, if you can finish it.) And good luck tackling Thomas Long, Haddon Robinson, Fred Craddock, Eugene Lowry, Henry Mitchell, John Stott, H. Grady Davis and Cleophus LaRue. Not to mention countless works by contemporary authors, all of whom have something to say about the process behind the presentation in the pulpit. Even for those who are the most dedicated to the improvement of their preaching, that is a lot of information to digest and apply. Indeed, mastering the theory behind homiletics seems reserved for the favored few who have the stamina for such in-depth study. This seemed like a job for the gifted.

This is what I came to believe. This is what I told myself years ago. I was unable to imagine how I could ever communicate God's word as effectively as those I most admired. As I left the campus church that evening all those years ago, I was convinced that I could never achieve those homiletical heights, because frankly, I was just too normal, and it was just too hard. Years later, I've come to realize that I wasn't entirely wrong. Doing what the great ones do IS hard. If we are going to be honest with ourselves, we would recognize that there are a few reasons why:

For starters, there is the matter of the **times** in which we live. The culture of the society in which we minister, and the culture of ministry have changed. Preaching is not a priority anymore. A 24-hour news cycle keeps us informed. Hundreds of television channels, as well as streaming services, keep us entertained. The rat race keeps us exhausted. Social media does much to keep us distracted. Worship services are now primarily driven by the need to get and hold the congregation's attention, as attention spans have significantly decreased. According to one study done by the Microsoft corporation, human beings generally lose focus after eight seconds. This gives us an attention span that is one second shorter than that of the average goldfish! We still haven't touched on the well-documented idea of Biblical illiteracy which suggests that, while most people are fond of the Bible, they don't actually read it, nor are they familiar with what it says. Not only is the average congregation not familiar with scripture, they are no longer convinced that the Bible should be the primary authority on how they live their lives. Nowadays, simply saying "The Bible says" and quoting scripture will no longer guarantee the preacher an audience as research shows that congregations are more inclined to employ their "confirmation bias" and interpret scripture based on what they already believe or find practically helpful. All of this makes preaching hard.

There's another layer to the difficulty of preaching. Preaching **theory** is not only dense but also disconnected. The sermon is one of the few methods of communication that remains stuck in the past and seems resistant to the changes that have affected the rest of the world. The internet in general, and social media in particular have required communication to be more portable. Twitter calls for soundbites while Instagram features filtered pictures with short captions designed to tell stories that stick. In order not to be lost in a sea of podcasts, videos, posts and pictures, your communication has to stand out and be noticed. Every preacher claims to receive a Word from God every seven days that stands in direct competition with a 24/7 news cycle and an Internet that never sleeps. All of this makes preaching hard.

In addition to all of the previously mentioned challenges, there is the issue of **time**. No matter how hard they try, most of the people called to preach just don't have unlimited time to prepare. Some who preach have families, school, jobs, and other responsibilities they have to manage. Others who are asked to preach work full-time jobs, have families and just want to preach effectively in addition to all of their other responsibilities. With careers, children, and other life challenges constantly battling for their attention, the average person finds it nearly impossible to set aside the exclusive quiet time it traditionally takes to create any noteworthy piece of art. Life gets the better of us, whether we are full-time or volunteer, and often it leaves us struggling the night before we have to mount the pulpit in search of a substantive message, we can deliver to the waiting congregation. It's not ideal. It's not fair. It is, however, a reality.

During the course of any given week the sermonic process can be attacked by any number of unscheduled and unforeseen predators. Attention stealers and time-wasters lurk around every corner just waiting for the opportunity to divert the preacher from the task at hand. Hardly a day goes by without something or someone that demands our time and divides our attention. Add to this the fact that the preaching we most often celebrate is done by guest speakers and is prepared and polished and practiced over a period of months instead of days. Your favorite sermon was probably preached at least a half-dozen times before you first heard it, which is one of the main reasons why it's so good! For the preacher who has to preach something brand new to the same congregation every weekend, creativity and consistency can prove to be a challenge. This makes preaching hard.

I'd like this book on preaching to approach the subject honestly. If we are going to be honest, we cannot ignore the matter of the individual preacher's **talent**. Interestingly enough, while people from all walks of life, from various cultures and backgrounds, with very different training and experiences have all been called to preach, we have not all been given the same gift of preaching. For some, preaching will not come easy. Everyone will not naturally prioritize and enjoy preaching. Some will preach better than others. That last statement can be potentially heart breaking if it's misunderstood…but please don't put the book down just yet! Any thoughtful and responsible communicator will want to improve and the people to whom we preach deserve our absolute best. However, our responsibility to give God OUR best should not be confused with a goal to be THE best. God reserves the right to distribute the preaching gift however God sees fit, and the gifts are not distributed evenly. The preacher can become intimidated by those with a different level or type of gifting instead of being faithful to the task at hand. Watching the gifts of others can leave you wondering whether the humble gifts you bring to the table are even worth sharpening to begin with. Sometimes you'll be tempted to give up sharpening them at all. That kind of thinking can make preaching hard.

One secret that is not often shared is that many of the most effective preachers often have the benefit of a **team.** Whether formally or informally, the best preachers are able to draw ideas from each other, bounce ideas off of each other, and in some cases work on entire sermons together! The preacher may stand behind the pulpit alone, but the sermon was definitely a team effort. Some preachers not only have teams who help find illustrations, check the sermon for cohesiveness and creativity, and feed them ideas, but they also scour books, videos, audio recordings and sermons heard in person for material, receiving assistance from their electronic "team". Chances are, you and I have listened to sermons "co-written" by some of the worlds most celebrated preachers without even knowing where these deep insights came from! If you are depending on your study and your study alone, without the assistance of either a physical or electronic community then you are fighting an uphill battle. This can make preaching hard.

The preacher deals with changing times, difficult theory, inconsistent preparation time, varying levels of talent and the absence of a team, not to mention additional obstacles. How exactly does one effectively preach? I want to propose a **technique** called, **Preach E.A.S.Y.** A simple, straightforward, system that will make it easier for the average person who preaches to consistently have something substantive to say while reducing the amount of preparation time it takes in order to say it well. This system allows you to "Effectively Authentically Share Your Story" (E.A.S.Y.) and is based on five foundational principles:

The gospel is the force that drives all E.A.S.Y. preaching. The gospel being front and center affects every aspect of the preaching event from communicator to content to congregation and is the only catalyst for genuine, lasting life-change.

The Bible is the foundation of all E.A.S.Y. preaching. Sermons grow directly out of the Biblical passage which ensures their power.

E.A.S.Y. preaching combines exposition and experience. That is to say, the sermon does more than repeat what the Bible says or explain what the Bible means. The preacher creates an experience using story throughout in an effort to show more than he or she says.

E.A.S.Y. preaching connects with people where they are, applying the Bible to the circumstances in which people live, using language people can easily understand.

E.A.S.Y. preaching communicates Biblical truth through each preacher's unique personality While the substance of the sermon is dictated by a study of scripture, sermon structure, stories told, and style of delivery are unique to each individual. This makes each sermon, "your story".

So many well-intentioned preachers find themselves dealing with the insecurity that comes along with staring down the road at an upcoming preaching moment and not having anything of substance to say. I believe this system will help. There are those who have great ideas that come from natural creativity or study and experience. You definitely have something to say, but you do not have the time to prepare to say it well. I believe this system can help you too. No matter where you fall on this spectrum, you are still called to preach. You are still given the mandate to spread the gospel. You have the privilege of working with heaven to share the good news of Jesus' love with His children here on earth. In spite of the changes in the church and the culture, you are not allowed to give up. You are called to preach. In spite of our limitations and our inadequacies, you are called to preach. Regardless of our circumstances and our individual challenges, you are called to preach. The call is non-negotiable. The gift is non-returnable. The mission is irresistible. This is why I am sharing this system. I believe that even though preaching gets difficult, we cannot give up on the task at hand. In spite of the obvious challenges that give us excuses why we shouldn't, there are also obvious reasons why we must:

We are all called to share the gospel. Whether as full-time clergy or everyday Christians, the great commission indicates that we are disciples who are called upon to preach. This is not a task left only to the gifted. It is a responsibility given to all.

This world is in desperate need. There are those who must be saved and quite frankly, the need is too great for the task to be left exclusively to those who have graduated from the Seminary. God has chosen the "foolishness of preaching" to accomplish the task and He expects all His servants at some point to be engaged. At some point, whether it's a small church or large, whether you were ever a theology student or not, you will be called to share the good news of God's word. Those upon whom God has laid this burden must respond.

To be clear, while there are those who preach because they are in love with preaching or because we love theory and theology, those who are called of God to preach respond because we love God's people! The people are the reason we prepare. The people are the reason we want to improve. The people are the reason the details matter. The people are the reason we preach!

God called us! Therefore, we have to preach, and we have to do it well! The people we serve deserve it. The times in which we live demand it. The God that we serve enables it. It's up to those who are given the task to step up to the plate and fulfill it. In my own search for a simple, time-saving system, I began to review the practices of preachers I admired the most. I took the time to research the preparation methods of over 30 of the world's most effective preachers and discovered that there were similarities in the way they all went about their business. I discovered that there were common principles that I or anyone who wants to preach effectively can put into practice and improve my preaching consistently. That discovery is the blessing I want to share with you. In an ideal world, it would be great to spend 40 hours each week studying and preparing to preach with no distractions whatsoever. To a bookworm like me, that sounds like heaven. For most who are reading this book, that will never be possible. We can, however, adopt the habits of those who preach consistently well, and use them to effectively, faithfully present the Word of God. Too often those who are tasked with explaining the art and science of preaching spend way too much time defending the complexity of their craft. I believe it's time to make sermon preparation simple, straightforward, and even enjoyable. I believe it's time to make sermons E.A.S.Y.

Here's a bird's eye view of where we're headed: Most approaches to sermon crafting are architectural or biological. Either the sermon is "constructed" or "developed organically". I propose another way of looking at the sermon that helps both the preacher and the people. I propose that the preacher take a journey in the pulpit that is shared with the people. Not only does this shared journey make preaching influential and impactful, I believe it also accomplishes one additional, critical goal. Sharing the journey makes things E.A.S.Y. Rather than "building" or "growing" a sermon, (The models with which most preachers are familiar) the preacher invites the congregation to travel with him or her through shared experiences that are familiar to them both, while preaching the good news that will impact them both. In order to make the journey meaningful, the preacher must make important decisions (such as where we are headed and why), map the journey (using your tools, knowledge and experiences) move the congregation toward the destination smoothly (selecting the appropriate vehicle, rest stops and route), and ensure that we arrive safely. A successful journey every time we communicate is our goal.

The best part about all of this is that none of it is complicated at all! The concept of a journey is familiar to everyone that has ever taken a trip, and anyone can put it into practice. Question: can you tell me where you live? Of course, you can! Just about everyone can give me directions to their home, and things would get even easier if I asked you to take me home with you. Many of you have driven down familiar roads towards home without even giving the directions a second thought! I believe we can share the Word of God in much the same way, and we don't have to look very far for advice on how to do it.

Jazz musicians are known for their improvisation. Listen to a jazz pianist and you'll be mesmerized by the creativity and expertise. Most onlookers focus on the fancy stuff without realizing that, in order to be that comfortable with creating, he or she had to first master the fundamentals. Once there is a basic system upon which the artist can build, talent and creativity can take over and produce something worth writing home about. This is the goal of Preach E.A.S.Y. This system provides a basic template that can be mastered then manipulated to allow the preacher's scholarship and creativity to shine.

In order to accomplish this, the book is divided into two parts: The first part covers the fundamentals and ensures that, whether you are a novice or an experienced professional, you can understand and utilize the preparation process to consistently have something Biblically-based and substantive to say. The second part of this book shares the outline I have developed in an effort to reduce the time it takes to organize your sermon effectively. The outline is made up of eight parts which will help every preacher connect with his or her congregation and call them to action. These steps are certainly not the only way to preach an effective sermon. However, mastering this method and adding it to your preparation routine will undoubtedly make preaching easier for you and listening easier for your congregation. The more comfortable you are with this process; the more freedom you will have to make these steps your own. Pretty soon, you will discover the same secret that I have: preaching does not have to be hard! I believe there is an alternative. I believe we can preach E.A.S.Y. By the end of this process, you will "Effectively Authentically Share Your Story".

Let's make this E.A.S.Y.

CHAPTER TWO

THE PROCESS

Preaching, as I mentioned before, is most effectively viewed as a journey. However, more needs to be said if we are to dive into a meaningful discussion of the process. In order to get the most out of this book, it's important that we first understand our purpose, our priorities, and the necessity of thorough preparation. This understanding will serve as the foundation for everything else that we will discuss. So, with that in mind, let's get started.

What Is Our Purpose?

I'm presenting a process, but the presentation would undoubtedly be more helpful if everyone understood the underlying reasoning. Without a clear reason behind the steps that are being taken, the steps will become debatable, and then eventually disposable as I eliminate whatever doesn't seem convenient at the time (and with busy schedules, we are always looking for a part of the process that we can eliminate).

I get it. Preachers nowadays just can't engage in the unnecessary. With someone or something always in competition for the limited time we have, we barely have time for the necessary, much less for the unnecessary. Wasting time is a luxury that productive people cannot afford, which is why every step in this process has to matter. Every assignment has to be purposeful. Every task has to bring us one step closer to the desired goal.

So that we can fully appreciate each step, we need to define the terms so that we are on the same page as it relates to what needs to be accomplished each and every time we declare the Word. Let's start by defining "preaching". The definition I crafted includes my non-negotiables. Not only are these non-negotiable for me, these are also the non-negotiables that I have observed in just about every effective preacher that I have ever heard preach and every effective sermon that

I have been blessed to preach. To be sure, my definition is not the only one, nor is it the most comprehensive definition of preaching. As a matter of fact, I'm certain that as soon as you read it, you will begin thinking of ways to improve upon my definition or even create your own. Let me encourage you to do just that! The art and science of preaching needs all of our perspectives and all of our contributions if it is going to thrive in the future. That being said, what follows is my definition of preaching so you can have an idea of what I used to keep myself on track:

> *"Preaching is a Spirit-empowered exercise that involves reaching back into the ancient text, pulling that text forward into the modern world, reaching across into people's lives, and pointing them upwards towards hope in Jesus."*
>
> – Gamal T. Alexander

These are the four basic purposes of every sermon. If the sermon has accomplished these objectives then, based on my observations, the sermon is a success. If, however, the sermon is lacking in any of these, then the sermon has fallen short overall. Effective preaching must accomplish all of these in order to be successful.

Notice how the definition begins. "Preaching is a Spirit-empowered exercise..." It's important to begin with this reminder because, in any technical discussion about preaching, I've found that the Spirit is much too easily forgotten. There is great danger in reducing preaching to nothing more than a process in an attempt to explain and master a task that only God can really perform. One of the characteristics that makes preaching different from other forms of communication is that, even when we have done all we can, we are still headed for guaranteed ineptitude without Divine power. We may accomplish other, lesser goals. We may encourage someone. We may excite someone. We may even manage to entertain. However, life change can only be accomplished if the Word that is preached is anointed by the Spirit of God. That is the only way. It is very possible to give a captivating talk, an informative presentation, or a persuasive speech and not have any lasting effect on anyone's spiritual life. Preaching, however, must be an entirely different matter. The heart change we are after requires the power of the One who created the human heart. The preacher needs the power of God's Holy Spirit above all.

Our definition continues: "Reaching back into the ancient text, pulling the text forward into the modern world, reaching across into people's lives, and pointing them upwards towards hope in Jesus". We realize that "reaching back" has to be the first responsibility of the faithful preacher, due to the nature of the Bible. While the Bible is certainly a book that is relevant right now, it is also a book of ancient origins. Written thousands of years ago, authored by people who lived millions of miles away, the Bible can seem very distant if we are not careful to bridge the gaps between "over there" and "over here".

Much of the cultural context of the Bible has long disappeared. The way people lived, what they ate, how they traveled, and even what they did for fun is foreign to us. That being the case, I suggest that a lot of what causes difficulty in interpreting and applying the Bible stems from the fact that the world of the Bible is "over there". In that world, women were treated poorly, money was valued, and wars were fought differently. Governments were run, people were transported, medicine was administered, and agreements were ratified differently. When we try to make a direct correlation, without bridging the gap, well-meaning preachers are often left saying to today's audiences something that the Bible just does not mean to say. When we handle God's Word irresponsibly, we eventually handle God's people irresponsibly. This is why we must be careful. We may think that it doesn't really matter, but biblical irresponsibility inevitably does God's people more harm than good.

Many students of scripture are to be commended for their faithful commitment to the study and understanding of the ancient texts. With an abundance of tools and thoughtfulness at their disposal, they have endeavored to uncover the hidden gems of meaning that often seem hidden within the pages of the Bible. These treasure hunters, who diligently dig up the meaning of the Biblical passage as the author intended when it was written, make sure that the congregation hears what the Bible meant to the audience who first heard it back then. This will undoubtedly fascinate any student of scripture. This will surely thrill the Bible scholar. It's always exciting to get as close as you possibly can to what the author was really trying to say. Keep in mind, however, that the people to whom we preach are not impacted by what the author meant back then. What informs their day to day decision-making is what the Bible means to the church that exists right now. The effective preacher must be careful to go a step beyond reaching back. The preacher must bring the Bible forward and also reach across.

A study of scripture that is restricted to history will go a long way toward informing us all about "them". At the conclusion of the study, I will know more about the Philistines and the Amalekites than I ever thought was possible. I can become an expert in the manners and customs, the characters and geography, and the authorial intent of every portion of the Bible. At that point I can be considered informed and maybe even intelligent. However, will my preaching have made an impact?

One way that I can guarantee that my preaching will remain irrelevant is by never making the connection between "them" and "us". At some point, I have to translate the information about how Lot made his decisions, into a sermon that influences how I make mine. I have to not only discover how God addressed the culture back then in Corinth and Ephesus, but as a preacher I must also determine what the author of the Bible has to say to individuals living in New York, Tampa, Baltimore, Dallas, Chicago, Portland, Denver, Charlotte, Cleveland, St Louis, Birmingham and Los Angeles. Does the Bible have anything to say about our relationships, our finances, our health and our futures? Yes, it does! As surely as the Bible spoke to "them" thousands of years ago, it speaks to "us" today. The job of the sermon is to make that connection. We reach back, pull forward, and reach across.

The preacher, however, is not finished reaching. Most modern preaching I believe, fails here. While many are careful to uncover the meaning of the ancient text and even more diligently connect the meaning of the passage to life in the present, preachers are unfortunately to often guilty of forgetting to point their congregations to Jesus. Sometimes Jesus accompanies our agendas. Sometimes Jesus plays second fiddle to our big ideas. I've been guilty of having something to say and finding text that supports my theory, all while saving Jesus for the grand finale as I come to the conclusion of my sermon and seek to somehow include the cross. Jesus, however, cannot play second fiddle, be second place, be relegated to second-class or be thought of as second rate. The Bible is God's book about Jesus. The congregation is gathered because they need Jesus. The object of our worship is Jesus and it is the preacher's responsibility to point thirsty souls to Him! No matter how eloquent, intricate, thoughtful, or technically sound, no sermon has adequately accomplished its mission unless it points the congregation to Jesus.

The Preacher's Priority
This definition leaves the preacher with a lot to accomplish. With a to-do list that long, we have to make sure we have our priorities straight!

First comes the process of preparation. That process begins not with the text, but with the preacher. God uses human beings to declare His word, and sometimes the dirt in those earthen vessels can get in the way. As a matter of fact, I'll take it one step further. If ever a sermon is ineffective, it's not God's fault. It's ours! Those who preach have this incredible ability to mess up every aspect of the sermon simply because it flows through us, and we are never enough. We are never smart enough, eloquent enough, sharp enough, patient enough, or skilled enough. We will never be enough, but we can give God more to work with. We do that by remembering the purpose of our task and making our preparation a priority.

"Making preaching a priority" sounds noble when it's written on paper. Priorities, however, are practical things. Priorities must be acted out and they must stand the test of time and life. This is where the rubber meets the road, and it is on this stretch of road where the preacher often stalls or breaks down altogether. As we all know, there are many factors that prevent us from making preaching a priority. Some of these distractions are more difficult to escape than others.

Many distractions are professional. When I first entered the ministry, I was under the impression that my primary responsibility was to preach (funny enough, everyone kept calling me a "preacher". Oh well…) I was led to believe that, since the expectations were that I would preach regularly and effectively, that the tools would be provided, resources would be allocated, and time would be designated for me to do my job.

Boy was I wrong.

Years later I've come to the realization that there was, at best, a catastrophic misunderstanding of the responsibilities of my role. What was made clear to me from the very beginning of my tenure, whether explicitly stated or implied, was that I may have been given the title "preacher", but preaching was often the last thing on my list of things that I was expected to do. Preaching was often thought of as this mystical art that, under the Spirit's guidance and with the Lord's help, would eventually take care of itself. According to this logic, God didn't necessarily need me to do more than jot down a few notes that He would email me throughout the week. (I never did get those emails. Maybe they wound up in the "junk" folder? Of course, this information would reach me before Friday when the church secretary usually requested the sermon text and title. During the week in my "spare time", I was to be occupied doing more important things. After all, people needed me! Come to think of it, the people need you too! There is vision to be cast and a sanctuary to be renovated. There is property to be purchased and there are evangelistic meetings to be run. There are administrative meetings to attend and paperwork to complete. What about the church school? Those poor children need you. What about the office? Thousands of people sit behind a desk and do paperwork every day. Shouldn't you? By the way, the phone is ringing. Aren't you going to return those calls? The congregation can benefit from your prayers, your visits, and your advice. The thing they need the least, it seems, is your preaching. At least, not until the weekend. And by then you'll definitely have it figured out (after all, YOU HAD ALL WEEK!). The problem with what I just described is that there is no part of my description that takes into consideration how the creative process works. As a matter of fact, this is not how the creative process has EVER worked. I have a confession to make. Somehow in my attempt to be "more than just preacher", I devolved into not being much of an effective preacher at all.

No description of the distractions would be complete if I didn't mention, once again, that many preachers approach the task all by themselves. Talk show hosts have teams that help to create content. Politicians and executives employ speech writers to help them compile information and craft effective presentations. Teams often offer feedback and constructive criticism. You, on the other hand, are expected to consult with God and God alone while desperately searching for the most memorable, impactful, remarkable way to tell a story that the congregation has heard at least a hundred times before. There are no editors, coaches, consultants, writers, producers, upon which we can depend and there are very few colleagues upon which we can lean (remember, your colleagues all have the same assignment due on the same day!). The preacher has to tackle the task of preaching without collaboration while being compared to television, YouTube, radio, and guest sermons that have been edited, massaged, practiced and polished before making it to our congregation's eyes and ears.

Of course, there is a measure of "help" available. If you want, preaching can be as easy as picking up a book of sermons or reworking a well-worn discourse you've preached before. Maybe you will see something on YouTube or come across something on television you can "borrow" for the weekend-so long as you promise to give it back. It's the night before preaching and all through the house…there's no time for prolonging the process. The shortcuts are always there. The temptation is always strong.

While many of the distractions that deter dynamic preaching are professional, we also have to admit that many distractions are personal as well. Ralph Waldo Emmerson lived in a cabin in the woods near Walden Pond so he could dedicate himself to his writing. Many creatives take writing retreats or buy studio time in order to birth their masterpieces. Even then, if they produce hit records or best-selling books every two or three years, they are considered genius. The preacher cannot remove his or herself from the hustle and bustle of life. Some would argue that to do this would rob the preacher of the connection with the people that informs powerful preaching. Still the preacher must continue to be faithful to family, friends, and community while also being faithful to the Word. The preacher is still a dad, mom, son, or a daughter. The preacher still gets sick, tired, depressed, lonely and burned out-all of which are factors that can affect creativity. The idea that the creative process begins automatically and continues undeterred as soon as the preacher makes the initial decision to complete the task is naive to say the least. To be honest, even if you do have the time, there is still one thing that can distract and deter you most from dynamic preaching. That "thing" is life!

Yet in spite of the pitfalls, preaching must remain a priority. It is not only the primary calling of the preacher, but according to scripture, the primary means by which men and women are brought to Jesus. "So, then Faith cometh by hearing and hearing by the Word of God." The Bible goes a step further…. "For without faith it is impossible to please the Lord". (Romans 10:17) Could it be that, by not prioritizing our preaching, we are short-changing believers of the faith necessary to please the Lord? Are we being unfaithful pastors, not by neglecting face-time with the people but by failing to prioritize the responsibility of preparing to preach? Preaching must become our priority, if for no other reason than God has ordained preaching as His priority. "It pleased God by the foolishness of preaching to save them that believe." (I Corinthians 1:21) If preaching is important to God, then it must be important to you and me. Making preaching important will always ensure that we have something to say.

The Task Of Preparation

This leads us to the task of preparation. If we believe that the purpose of preaching is much more than inspiration or religious entertainment, that preaching involves bridging the gap between what happened in the Bible "over there" and what's happening in our world "over here", and if we believe that we preach in the face of distractions of every kind and yet we must preach because precious lives depend on our preaching then our top priority must be proper preparation. Regardless of the obstacles that stand in front of us, or the difficulties that arise within us, we must ensure that we produce consistently effective preaching. Every time there is an opportunity to share God's word, it must be done with excellence. The next chapter will point us in the right direction as we seek to do just that.

CHAPTER THREE

SO IT BEGINS!

A friend of mine recently posted a confession on social media, and honestly I think most preachers can relate. It was about a sermon he recently preached. According to him, even though God blessed the message he preached, he knew within himself once he was finished, that he could have done so much more. God had done God's part, but the preacher had left so much on the table. The pastor found himself torn. The sermon could have been more effective had he been more diligent. God did His part, but this preacher had not done his, and he knew that God's people deserved better.

I happen to agree.

God desires to partner with us in the preaching moment to share the story of His love. In this partnership, God (the Senior Partner) gives us the inspiration and the benefit of divine insight that ensures the effectiveness of the sermon. God tells the preacher what to preach, all the while aligning the message with the hearts of people that He has been working on all week. To be sure, God never fails in doing His part, but God will force you to have a solid plan. While it is through the "foolishness of preaching" that God has determined to save men and women, effectiveness requires that preaching not be executed foolishly. God and the preacher must work together. My friend on Facebook said it best: "God's got the message, I'm responsible for the sermon".

I've got bad news: the weekend is coming, and the sermon isn't going to write itself. The news gets worse: God isn't going to write it for you either. Not to worry. Those best practices that the most effective preachers employ in order to preach life-changing sermons are packaged here for you. The "E.A.S.Y." system is designed to take the preacher from concept to full-fledged sermon. Mind you, these techniques are not unique. They are born of an interdisciplinary approach that incorporates everything from standup comedy, to TED talks, to classical preaching. These principles and practices also come from different cultures and span different eras. Some of the practices you will be familiar with. Some of the terminology you have heard before. What's more, if you have ever heard an effective sermon preached, then you have undoubtedly seen these principles in practice. The principles that make up the E.A.S.Y. system are not obscure; and neither is the research behind them. Most of these best practices come from books that most preachers have at least skimmed before. However, even if you've never heard of the literature that supports these best practices, know that these principles have worked countless times for speakers from all walks of life and they will work for you. Just know, however, that there is no magic formula. Rather, there is a method that is intended to accomplish the purpose of taking the sting out of preparation. Before I tell you "how" it works, let me tell you why:

The E.A.S.Y. System Works Because It's Liberating.

The system works by outlining a set preparation process and presenting a template that can be used to create sermon outlines. There are also guidelines on what to do in order to fill in the remaining information. This allows the preacher to spend time on other areas that will make the sermon more unique. Instead of wondering what an effective introduction should look like, why not focus on finding effective illustrations? Instead of debating what details to highlight from the text, why not focus on stating each point in a way that the congregation can remember and repeat? The system gets the preacher past the usual sticking points, which frees the preacher to do other important, creative things.

The E.A.S.Y. System Works Because It Is User-Friendly.

Simply put, the system was made for the preacher, not the preacher for the system. Rather than be dogmatic about how sermons should be prepared, I'm proposing a system that can be tailored to meet the preacher's needs. Whether you are preaching an evangelistic sermon, a pastoral sermon, a sermon that is a part of a series, a sermonette directed at youth or young adults, a funeral, wedding or a conference attended by thousands, this system can help you effectively, authentically share your story. The process is straightforward and the outline is simple, yet they can be used in just about every preaching situation to communicate effectively. You can use the process just about anywhere once you've made the process your own.

The E.A.S.Y. System Will Work Because It Is Logical.

The sermon is no longer the primary medium that shapes Christian values. Question the membership of any church and you will discover that there is stiff competition for access to their minds and hearts. Everything from Twitter to Television plays an important role in shaping what we believe and how we live out that belief in our everyday lives. These tweets, TED talks, Podcasts, Facebook posts, YouTube videos, Google searches, and Talking Heads all have effective methods of communicating that condition on how your congregation receives and remembers information. Isn't it logical to learn?

This is what Preach E.A.S.Y. attempts to do. This system takes into consideration classical homiletic theory and emerging trends and merges the most important lessons from both. Preaching cannot afford to be stuck in the cultural vacuum created by a bygone era. The Gospel is too important for that. We must be willing to sacrifice our sacred cows upon the altar of continuing education as we affirm our commitment to fulfill our Great Commission- and go.

Mastering this system, and making it a consistent part of your routine, will pay dividends when it comes to the effectiveness of your preaching. That being said, this is far from the only way to prepare and preach sermons. There are countless books, numerous ideas, and many other methods out there. Explore them, master them, and use them! The more tools you have in your toolbox, the better.

And speaking of tools, let's begin unboxing ours...

Tool One: Saturation

> *"You cannot inspire others unless you are inspired yourself."*
> CARMINE GALLO

Consider this: before you even enter the study and determine what text to preach on, you have already determined whether or not you have anything of worth to say. The study and research will ultimately determine the content of the sermon, but it is your passion that will ignite the flames. We can only make withdrawals from an account that we have deposited into, which is why mastery of the Bible, as well as a thirst for information in general, will be the biggest contributor to our success in the pulpit. Having a full tank of information goes a long way towards making the preaching journey easier, and passion drives us to constantly fill the tank. This is because passion leads to mastery. Passion inspires us to keep reading and drives us to continue listening. Passion requires us to keep working and ensures that we don't stand in front of our congregations and attempt to share from intellectual accounts that have insufficient funds.

One of the most influential platforms used to spread ideas is the "TED Talk". Even people who are not inclined to listen to sermons will view a TED Talk in a positive light. They are always short (no more than 18 minutes in length), delivered conversationally, and they touch on a wide range of ideas. They are considered to be the modern standard for effective communication. In his book, "Talk Like TED", Carmine Gallo says, "The most popular TED speakers share something in common with the most engaging communicators in any field – a passion, an obsession that they must share with others. These people are called to share their ideas." What ideas are you called to share? Discovering these requires thought, and intelligent thought is driven by information. This concept is foundational to any presentation and is also very difficult to achieve consistently. Most preachers succumb to the temptation of preaching sermons that are ill-informed and not clearly thought out. That kind of preaching must be avoided at all costs. Thinking IS hard work. (If you don't believe that thinking is difficult, just look around and take note of all the people that refuse to do it every day!) However, if you and I are going to speak effectively, we need to spend the necessary time doing the heavy lifting of preparing our minds before we open our mouths. This kind of heavy lifting is a lot easier when you have a "S.P.O.T.E.R."

Using The "S.P.O.T.E.R."
Aristotle is quoted as saying, "We are what we repeatedly do. Excellence, then, is not an act but a habit." Researchers Jim Loehr and Tony Schwartz have this to say, "As little as 5 percent of our behaviors are consciously self-directed. As creatures of habit, as much as 95% of what we do is habitual." With this in mind, the answer to the question of excellent preaching has to involve creating habits that consistently produce effective sermons and continually prepare excellent preachers. Good sermons then, are the product of good habits that are formed away from

the pulpit which will, in turn, shape the presentation in the pulpit. I've created the acronym "S.P.O.T.E.R." to describe the habits that I discovered from my research to be the most beneficial to the effective preacher. (In case you were wondering, I am fully aware that "S.P.O.T.E.R." is spelled incorrectly. The correct spelling of the word would not have fit the acronym. That being said, I did win a spelling bee in the 6th grade, so there's that...)

Using the S.P.O.T.E.R. as a checklist, the preacher can ensure that whether they preach often or inconsistently, whether they are busy or on vacation, they are constantly making deposits into their intellectual banks that will always ensure that when the time comes, they will have something to say. Let's take a closer look at the six questions the "S.P.O.T.E.R." asks of us: (In no particular order...)

1. Have I studied?
2. Have I prayed?
3. Am I observant?
4. Am I thinking?
5. Am I exposing myself to new things?
6. Am I being renewed?
7. Have I studied?

The Bible is the preacher's primary workbook, yet there are those who intend to preach from it and yet they have not familiarized themselves with what it says. It stands to reason that, for those who would endeavor to talk to people about the God of the Bible and what God says in the Bible, it would be of the utmost importance to actually know the Bible. Granted, no one can be expected to memorize every chapter and every verse. What's more, the internet makes information accessible which can help just about anyone find their way around the Word. Still, preachers often fall into the danger of knowing more about the culture around them and the condition of the people in front of them than they do about the Bible that contains the answers for the culture and the people. To know the culture and not know the Bible is to reduce one's preaching to mere social commentary. To know people and not know the Bible is to traffic in pulpit psychology. The preacher must know the Bible and know it well enough to quote it, interpret it, and apply it appropriately. According to Paul's advice to Timothy, the preacher should be able to rightly divide the word of truth. (2 Timothy 2:15) This level of comfort and familiarity with scripture does not happen overnight, nor does it come without sacrifice. In fact, one can spend a lifetime studying the scriptures and still be confident that he or she has not even scratched the surface. When it comes to the Word of God, our people have a lot to learn. As it turns out, so do we.

Types Of Bible Study

Not only is the Bible an inexhaustible textbook available for our study, but there are also multiple ways of approaching the task. A quick Internet search will reveal a half dozen or more methods of Bible study that all promise results. Based on methodology from the book, "Rick Warren's Bible Study Methods", here are methods of Bible study that are sure to be effective for the preacher who is determined to be a dedicated student of God's Word:

Devotional study. At the very least, every Christian should spend some time each day meditating on the Word of God and listening for what the Bible has to say with regard to his or her life. I believe that a daily quiet time or devotional time should be a practice of every believer. As a matter of fact, I believe in the practice so strongly that, to date, I have published two devotional workbooks of my own (Faith 2.1 and Grace 2.1 available at www.gamalalexander.com). Most people don't have the time to transform morning devotions into in-depth study, but there is still much to be gained from consistent exposure to God's Word. Here is one format to add to your arsenal that will help get your day started off right:

1. *Talk to the Lord (Pray)*
2. *Think it over (Meditate)*
3. *Take notes (Applications)*
4. *Take it to heart (Internalize a scripture)*

Starting every day like this will inevitably yield positive results. A consistent habit of internalizing scripture and writing down personal applications will ensure that there are ideas from which you can draw and explore should you need to use them in the future.

Other types of study. Along with devotional study, there are at least five other methods of systematic Bible study in which the preacher can engage. One of the many benefits of consistent study is the luxury of having information at your disposal when needed. Rather than having to research facts about Peter or texts about the Grace of God, the preacher is already familiar with these subjects and simply preaches from the overflow of his or her knowledge and experience. Here are five incredibly effective ways to head start the process of preparation.

1. **Topical study.** *Select a topic such as "Forgiveness" or "Faith" and, using a concordance, study the text and scripture associated with the topic. Should you ever be called upon to preach on the topic, you will never have to worry about finding appropriate scriptures from which to preach.*
2. **Text by Text chapter study.** *Allowing the Bible to be its own interpreter, the preacher can take the opportunity to study Biblical truth in the context of the chapter in which it was written.*
3. **Character study.** *Select a Bible character such as "Timothy" or "Moses" and study everything associated with his life. This study can be especially exciting as there are Bible characters that are often seen as insignificant that hold valuable lessons for God's people.*
4. **Word study.** *The word "sin" in scripture is packed with meaning. Other words, such as "perfect" are often misunderstood. The preacher that seeks to responsibly handle scripture would do well to familiarize his or herself with these nuances on a regular basis.*
5. **Book study.** *The book of Romans has been a blessing to many. Why not allow it to bless you and your congregation? The book of Esther never once mentions the name of God, yet God's presence is felt from beginning to end. Have you discovered what lessons that fact holds for you and for those to whom you preach?*

Building the habit of consistent private study will yield dividends in the pulpit. This is a habit worth developing. However, study should not be limited to the Bible if the preacher wishes to be effective. One of my favorite quotes from Virginia Woolf puts it this way, "Read a thousand books and your words will flow like a river." Study a wide range of topics. Read a wide variety of books. Discover how others express their ideas. Learn about how others solve life's problems. From books to blogs and everything in between, there is a wealth of information that can help any preacher learn and grow. Whether it's the "Good Book" or a good book, a part of the preacher's routine has to include consistent and varied reading.

Have I Prayed?
One of the first Christian disciplines to be crowded out of the daily

routine is prayer. Yet prayer has been described as, "the breath of the soul". No one in their right mind would go into the daily battle without breathing, yet we often attempt to share the gospel without first being covered in prayer! The preacher must remember that the act of preaching is itself spiritual warfare as captives are being liberated. With the enemy standing in direct opposition at all times, the preacher needs all the strength he or she can get.

The Bible describes one of the roles of the Holy Spirit as, "guiding people into all truth." Preachers are dedicated to making the truth plain, but the Spirit-guided preacher receives the truth from the Lord, as well as the power to share that truth, which is in turn shared with the people. Prayer endows the preacher the power not only to convince the hearer of the information, but also convict the heart which prepares the way for the sermon. Prayer removes the obstacles and distractions and prepares both preacher and people to experience the message rather than just listen. That's the very thing that needs to be accomplished in order for lives to be changed.

Am I Observant?

What are you looking at? From mother nature to human nature, from sports and popular culture to the classics and figures of yesteryear, there are shared life experiences that can be used to illustrate Biblical principles. We can find them if we would simply pay attention. The preacher should be mindful of his or her surroundings, because as you are journeying through life you are sharing experiences every day to which your congregation can relate. God could have drafted angels to descend from heaven and preach the gospel. Instead He uses human beings to share the good news. One of the reasons why He does this, I believe, is because we can relate to each other. We speak a language that our brothers and sisters understand. When Jesus came to the earth, "the Word was made flesh and dwelt among us". (John 1:14) When we pay attention to the ups and downs of everyday life and utilize them in our preaching, we allow our sermons to undergo an incarnation of sorts. Our preaching sends the clear message that, "This helped me, and it can help you, because I am just like you. We are all in this together."

Am I Exposing Myself To New Things?

I believe that the preacher should be a lifelong learner. I won't go so far as to encourage you to follow every fashion and latest fad, but exposure to new concepts, ideas, technology, and ways of communicating can go a long way in helping us find new ways to tell the old, old story. It can also go a long way towards improving the preacher. Research suggests that Continuing to challenge the brain serves as a protection against life-related mental decline. Technology, in particular, has made great strides in facilitating our continuing education. Whether formally or informally, there's almost no limit to what the preacher can learn. The library, the internet, travel and life experiences can go a long way towards expanding the mind. And speaking of expansion, may I suggest that preachers be intentional about exposing themselves to new subject matter? The temptation to stay within our informational comfort zone definitely exists. If we are not careful, most preachers will read books and journals about the Bible, theology, preaching, leadership and self-improvement without ever exposing themselves to something new. Meanwhile, a standup comedian and the biography of a professional athlete might help your preaching just as much as a book on leadership or practical theology. Don't sell yourself short. Don't cut yourself off. Take some chances and expose yourself to something new!

Eventually, you will be able to develop the skills to present your familiar subject in a way that is fresh and new. And nothing is more impactful than information that is packaged differently or reveals a fresh and creative way of solving a problem.

Am I Being Renewed?

I can't think of a better way to sharpen the tools of communication than to periodically give the communicator a rest. For those who have the difficult task of thinking for a living, practicing self-care and occasionally hitting the "relax" and "reset" buttons is always a good idea. Especially when you find yourself getting stuck. Whether it's a hobby you enjoy, a book you read, a conversation that revives you, or just taking time to have fun, productivity and creativity are enhanced when we take time out to unplug.

A recent Gallup poll suggests that one of the key factors in sustained performance is having at least one friend at work. Why? Because we are simply more productive when we take time to play. Excellence is achieved more easily when we are enjoying ourselves. Whether it takes the form of a vacation or a consistent day off, make sure you get away from the constant creative grind, turn your mind off, and give yourself a break. Get some exercise. Visit your therapist. Sit in silence and enjoy your own company. STOP PRODUCING! The benefits to creativity of consistent renewal are well worth the effort, resources, and energy we invest.

Step Two: Sit

One of the most frustrating aspects of the creative process is that it cannot be rushed. Sometimes the preacher has to sit on good ideas until they are ready, which is why preparation for every sermon MUST BEGIN long before you ever have to preach! Every preacher has had the hair-raising experience of racing against a deadline and having to deliver a message regardless of whether or not they were fully prepared. That happens to the best of us and sometimes it's unavoidable. It seems as if the weekend is always just around the corner and our pulpit appointments cannot be postponed for anyone. Ready or not, here it comes! Thankfully, we have all had the experience of seeing God come through at the last minute. I can personally testify to having nothing of substance to say just before the preaching moment and feeling led to write down a few bullet points on a church bulletin, or work through a main idea on the way to church. I know that God has blessed, I have seen how God has blessed, and I am sure that God can bless.

I can also assure you that those sermons were not my best work. Not by a long shot.

Grace is so abundant and mercy so amazing that we tend to take both for granted. Yet, God still gives new starts and second chances. The issue here, however, is not our presentation but our potential. When we do the minimum necessary to get by, we rob ourselves of the opportunity to have God do His best through us! Could it be that God desires to use you just as effectively as He uses the preacher you most admire? Is He waiting for you to dedicate the time and discipline necessary for Him to you use the way God really wants to? Is it possible that what separates you from the preachers you most admire is not the amount of spare time or the library they have access to, but the fact that they have consistently good habits of preparation that give these preachers the time and space to think through great ideas until those ideas are clear?

Here's another question: Have you ever listened to a preacher and wondered, "How did they come up with that?" or "Where did they find that?" You know that they are reading the same Bible and studying the same text that you have read time and time again, and yet what they are sharing sounds so creative, fresh and thoughtful. Why? These preachers give themselves the time and space to converse with the text and discover the answers to their questions that lie below the surface. Being in a rush to write often means having to rehash many of the same things you have heard before. No wonder we are still telling the same jokes! Daniel's friends are still, "Shadrach, Meshach and A-bad-negro", because we don't have the time and space to think of anything new! You can't rush genius. Big ideas often come to the unconscious mind.

So, how exactly do we go about the business of sitting? Look at the way your days and weeks are set up. As a matter of fact, take a step back and look at your yearly calendar. When is there time for serious planning, creating, or dreaming? Are you always writing or speaking? Have you given yourself the time and space to think of something new? Do you have the time to ask yet another question of the text? Do you have the time to reject your first conclusions and challenge yourself to look at the passage in a different way? Can you afford to reshape the main idea because you've thought about it and realized that it doesn't connect with anything else in the sermon, or with you? Will you give yourself the opportunity to go into deeper Bible study because you realize that the conclusion you've reached really isn't what the Bible is trying to say?

As we create, waiting is sometimes just as important as writing. If not more so. Whether we have selected our themes and texts well in advance so we have time to allow the ideas to marinate, or the texts are selected at the beginning of the week to give ourselves the breathing room needed to take a deeper look, one thing is certain: The successful preacher cannot race against the clock and consistently create something of quality. I don't care what method you use or what the latest preaching book promised you. Great preaching just doesn't work that way. We are often in a hurry to record what God wants to say, while God is not in as much of a hurry to speak to us. Instead, He carefully allows His word to take root in our hearts, and His ideas to develop in our minds. Give yourself the time and space to wait for God to speak. Remember, good things come to those who wait.

The pre-work has been completed, but our appointment with the pulpit is still approaching. Thankfully, your saturation and your sitting have given you the beginnings of an idea. Now it's time for you to do the necessary work that enables you to communicate that idea to the masses. Not to worry, this process takes us from the study to the sanctuary. There is much more to come.

The fun is just getting started!

CHAPTER FOUR
TREASURE HUNTING

I once heard someone say that the preacher has two temptations to avoid. The first is to talk about the Bible to the people. This preacher is well-researched and his or her conclusions are well thought out. However, while the congregation will learn everything there is to know, and about everything the Bible says, the preacher will never get around to sharing what the Bible has to say to them. The second temptation is to talk about the people using the Bible. This preacher knows everything there is to know about culture, psychology, and the human condition. They can masterfully utilize the preaching moment to dispense relationship counseling, financial advice, and wisdom on everything from conflict resolution to peaceful living. The preacher can advocate for social justice, argue for prison reform and decry the evils of voter registration all while encouraging men to be good fathers and women to realize their God-given independence. The congregation would DEFINITELY leave with a load of helpful information. However, none of it has to necessarily have anything to do with the Bible. Worse yet, the preacher can press the Bible into the service of supporting his or her agendas while never discovering the message God actually has for His people from the Word. A solid sermon preparation process is necessary to avoid these two extremes. Rather than talk about the Bible to the people, or talk to the people using the Bible, sermon preparation ensures that we talk about what God has to say to the people through the Bible. This is how we know that our congregations will be more than just informed or inspired. By the end of the sermon, our congregations should be impacted and influenced towards radical life change.

Step Three: Search
Every so often, a media outlet has to post a disclaimer before airing a program, in order to shield themselves from being labeled as sharing the

views of those who are about to be speaking during their airtime. We're all familiar with a statement that reads something like, "The views and opinions expressed in this program do not necessarily reflect the views of the organization…" Sometimes websites, television shows, and other outlets need to run those disclaimers in order to let the audience know that the person speaking, is coming up with the content on their own.

I think some preachers could use that disclaimer too.

We have all seen Biblical texts that were used as launching pads for the burden the preacher had on his or her heart, or to advance the agenda the preacher had on his or her mind. Truth be told, the preacher didn't really need the text for anything more than the license to call the presentation a sermon! There was no attempt made to discover what the Bible was trying to say and no link to what the Bible actually said. It was as if the preacher forgot that the text was even there.

I guess we should still count our blessings. Things could always be worse.

We have all witnessed the Biblical texts that were kidnapped and forced into slavery. The Bible clearly did not want to go, and clearly did not belong where it was sent. Nevertheless, tyrannical homiletic overlords pressed the Biblical passages into service and made the Bible say things that it was never intended to say. Some texts suffered a horrible fate as they were made to endorse heresy, create division, support discrimination and injustice against their will. Those poor texts have been made to do unspeakable things, and it could have all been avoided.

I believe that the Bible is relevant simply because it houses the truth of God's word. It doesn't have to be made relevant. It is relevant. It doesn't need to be modernized, nor does anything have to be added to its pages to make the scripture more effective. With the Bible, we have all we need. The problem at times is that we don't always understand everything we have. Written thousands of years ago in a very different world, with different cultural norms, and different values, our misinterpretation of writing that was not originally meant for us to read can lead to trouble. Well-meaning preachers seeking desperately to be relevant, often preach the Bible as if it was written "over here" in Bermuda in 2019 when in fact the last books of the Bible were written centuries ago before Bermuda ever existed.

In order for us to fully and responsibly comprehend what the Bible is saying to God's people "over here", we have to first determine what it meant to the people it was originally written for "over there". This process is called exegesis. Not only is it vitally important for proper interpretation and responsible application, but it can also provide details about the passage that will help it come alive. During the process of exegesis, we ask certain questions about the passage, recipients, and author in order to determine what the Bible was originally trying to say. We do more than just ask questions of the text. (Questions like, "Who wrote it and why?) We also ask questions about the text. (Questions like, "Why is that word placed there and what does it mean?") Once we have unearthed all of the information, we can reasonably discover about what the text meant to those who wrote it and first heard it (keeping in mind that we can never find infallible answers because, well, we can't ask Moses or Paul) we are then free to determine what the passage should mean to us. All of this is involved in the process I refer to as "searching."

Here are the steps involved in "Searching":

1. *Read the text in as many versions as possible, and as many times as necessary. I read the passage in at least the KJV, NKJV, NIV, NRSV, NASB, ESV, Amplified, the Message Bible, the New Century Version and Young's Literal Translation before I get started.*
2. *Make an outline of the events of the story or paraphrase the text in your own words. I want to be familiar with the details.*
3. *Record initial observations about the text.*
4. *Begin to ask and answer questions about the passage and the people involved. Who wrote this? Who was first exposed to this? When was it written? Why was this written? What could it have meant to those who read it? How must they have felt? How must the writer have felt?*
5. *Note key words in the passage that grab your attention, particularly verbs. He "ran". She "fell on her face". Pay attention. That's where the action is!*
6. *Use Bible dictionaries, commentaries and online resources to study the background, culture, and setting. You want to know as much about the author, recipients, and the situation surrounding the passage as possible.*
7. *Using a concordance, cross-reference the passage under consideration with other scriptures.*
8. *Use commentaries to compare and contrast initial observations. The best commentaries will also add additional insight to my research.*
9. *Consult additional resources such as devotional writings and other sermons.*
10. *Write a short paragraph that answers three important questions: What is*

this passage originally trying to say? What problem was it trying to solve? Is there a lesson for me today?

These questions will begin to help the preacher discover what the passage was originally intending to say and avoid the pitfalls of saying something that the Biblical writers never meant to convey. The most effective preachers, however, don't stop here. They go beyond the initial questions and ask even deeper ones about the text under consideration. Here are a few "second-tier" questions that I have come across:

1. Is there anything peculiar about the author?
2. Are there any noticeable circumstances surrounding the recipients?
3. Are there any special circumstances surrounding when and why the passage was written?
4. Was there anything special happening in the world when the passage was written? (The passing of a king, a new ruler taking the throne, and kingdom being conquered)
5. What was life like in that part of the world?
6. What helpful information does a study of the characters involved provide? (Peter was a fisherman. What was life like for them? What tools did they use? How did they do their work?)

The answers to these and other questions should yield plenty of background information about the type of world in which the text was written and the circumstances surrounding the passage. Remember, the characters in the Biblical stories lived in a world with which we are not familiar. If you're going to introduce these foreigners to your congregation, then your people will need as much information as possible to make these characters relatable and familiar. This context helps us to fill in the blanks about who the people of the Bible were and how they lived. Keep in mind that some Biblical stories were recorded well after the events actually happened which puts even more distance between what happened and where we are today. Understanding the author's world as well as the context of the events in the text will provide some much-needed perspective.

Using free online resources like Biblehub.com and Bible Gateway as well as the Strong's Concordance, commentaries like the IVP Background Commentary, Word Pictures in the New Testament, the Complete Word Study Dictionary of the Old and New Testament, Manners and Customs of the Bible, devotional readings, books, articles, and other available resources, will help you gather useful information about your text. While a local Bible college or Seminary library will have everything you need, free of charge, investing in your commentaries as well as the logos Bible software would definitely make things more convenient.

That being said, Google still works.

By now, quite a bit of research has been done. However, we are not done because there are details that we haven't found yet. Our goal is to become experts on this passage. This doesn't mean we're writing a dissertation or getting an advanced degree. It does mean, however, that we intend to know just as much if not more about this passage than our listeners do. You and I are going to gather as much relevant information as possible WITHOUT being overwhelmed. An interesting sermon doesn't require the preacher to use everything he or she finds. Still, the more you investigate, the more intimate you and your story will become, and the more authentically you will be able to tell the Biblical story. You will tell the Bible story as if you've been there because in a sense, as a result of your research, you HAVE been there. So here are some details you will want to consider locating during your research:

1. **Meanings of names.** *Do the names of the people or places in the passage have any significance?*
2. **Recurring locations or repeated circumstances.** *Does this place look familiar? Where have you encountered this person, place, or circumstance elsewhere in the Bible? If you have seen this happen before, or if you have seen this person before, you should probably take a closer look.*
3. **Background information on auxiliary characters.** *These people (or even animals) may not be the stars of the show, but they are mentioned for a reason. What are they doing? Why are they there? Maybe they can teach us something.*
4. **The genre of the passage.** *Is this passage a poem? Prophecy? A proverb? A historical record? Is the language here literal or figurative? The type of literature we are reading will often give clues as to how we should interpret what we are reading. The flowery, figurative language of a poem cannot be interpreted in quite the same way as a wisdom saying (a proverb) or a historical record. Once again, pay attention. These important details matter.*

The details are important, but we can't get so caught up in the details we discover, that we forget where the passage fits in the overall scheme of scripture. This passage is a part of a chapter, which is part of a book, which is part of the Bible. When we are determining the context of the text in question, we cannot claim to completely understand unless we have understanding on every level. Even if we don't have time to explain it or expound on it, we need to fully understand everything that we are reading.

Our goal is to understand the immediate context. Our research should lead us to understand how this passage fits into the chapter it came from. By the time you are ready to preach, you should be familiar with the text you are studying as well as the verses preceding and following the text. That lowers the chances of gross misappropriation.

The preacher should also understand the context of the book. What is the significance of this text in light of the book of which it is a part? Is it the introduction to a letter? Is it a part of a larger story? Understanding the place of the passage in the book lowers the chance of misinterpretation.

Lastly, the preacher should understand the canonical context. Where does this text fit in the grand scheme of scripture? Is this text a prophecy yet to be fulfilled? Is this text a matter of record that has already been fulfilled? Is this a promise God made in the past? Is God making this promise to everyone? Understanding the context of the passage in light of the entire Bible lowers the chance of misapplication.

Once you've explored the context and discovered what the Bible writer was trying to say, begin to narrow your focus by asking additional questions about what you are reading. There's a rhyme I learned in elementary school that seems like a great fit here:

> "I had six faithful friends, they taught me all I knew.
> Their names were how and what and why,
> when and where and who."

Answering those questions gives additional intent into what the author was saying and the reasons behind what is being said. The continued investigation inevitably leads to additional insight.

Now that we have gone treasure hunting, it's time to take a step back and make sense of what we have found. The searching process will lead us, in the next step, to sift through all of the information we've gathered and distill that information into the idea the preacher wants the congregation to know more than anything else. We're definitely making progress, but the process is far from over. Before we move on from our searching, we should be able to answer Haddon Robinson's two very important questions:

1. What exactly was the Biblical writer talking about?
2. What was the Biblical writer saying about it?

The lessons within the text may be fascinating, but they don't connect just yet. Not to worry. There's a lot more for us to see.

Step Four: Sift

Do you see it? Of course, you do! There it is! We have now discovered the intent of the author. Identify it, and make sure it is true. However, our work is not done because this is not an exegesis paper, it's a sermon. So far, we have done enough research to ensure that we are faithful to the text, but we have not done enough work to ensure that we are connecting the text to our listeners. Now we have to move from searching to sharing. It's time to pass this information through filters until we have one central idea that we can call our own. But how? After all, there's so much out there about the Amalekites. Who knew?

Not so fast! While you and I may be amazed by the wealth of information about our subject, our listeners won't be as interested or impressed. The average congregant doesn't have the same fascination or interest level about the subject as we do. While Biblical characters and backgrounds may excite us, it's practical Biblical principles that get our listener's attention. Although, we may be fascinated by how the people of the Bible lived back then, our listeners are more interested in what God has to say about living for Him today. That's why the sermon is far from complete. We are responsible for making this teaching from the Word of God clear. This means that it's up to us to organize and present the information in such a way that everyone, regardless of interest or comprehension level, can understand and apply it. This is a tall order that requires the sermon to be more than just informative. The sermon has to be interesting, practical, attention-grabbing, and helpful. In order to achieve any of those things, the sermon has to be focused. It has to communicate only one message. It has to say just one simple thing. This is where the next step comes in. This is where we discover the idea that your sermon will deposit into their brains. This is where we make the transition from researching the facts to reaching the people.

It's time to craft our central idea.

Chris Anderson, the curator of TED, the organization responsible for the world-famous TED Talks, is quoted as saying, "If you cannot express an idea in one sentence then you are not ready to share that idea." I wholeheartedly agree with him. Too many sermons have ambitiously tried to accomplish multiple goals, while failing to accomplish any. The people who listen to us do not have the time or the patience to decipher what we are trying to communicate, nor do they want the responsibility of tracking us through the jungle of our many great ideas. In order to make the sermon clear and memorable, the preacher must determine what ONE THING he or she will leave with the people. The "central idea", as I like to call it, should be related to the information found in the text that you've previously chosen.

Simply put, the key is to present just one idea as thoroughly and completely as you can in the limited time period. What is it that you want your audience to have an unambiguous understanding of after you're done? That's the question answered by the central idea. The central idea traces the path your sermon will take, ensuring that the path is creative, concise, and clear. This central idea takes you one step closer to the goal of saying something meaningful.

The central idea is a succinct statement that conveys your overall message. Based on what your study has shown you about what the Bible originally meant, you should now be able to create that sentence in a way that answers these two questions:

1. "What am I talking about?"
2. "What am I saying about it?"

The answer to these questions should be contained in one short statement, of 15 words or less, which will then serve as the basis for everything that we will preach from now until the end of the sermon. Creating the sentence from the answers to these questions is our primary concern as we forge ahead. Every point you preach will flow from this central idea. Every illustration will illuminate this central idea. This idea comes directly from the text and is what holds the sermon together. Once you have the thematic sentence, you have a foundation from which you can continue your work to create an outline.

Remember, the central idea must be about ONE thing! The human mind appreciates linear thought and cannot remember scattered ones. Often, our minds are too distracted and the allotted time too limited for any preacher to do justice to complex ideas and multiple texts. The limit of saying just one thing forces the preacher to be more concise and makes the preacher concentrate, as well as be more creative. Research has shown that structure and restriction do lead to creativity.

The central idea is being crafted, which is the idea that I want to communicate. This is the idea that I am building my sermon around. I want to keep it relatable, simple and memorable. After all, I want my central idea to be actionable! The goal is not for the preacher to show how much he or she knows about a text or a given subject, but rather, the goal is to share a lesson that sticks, and produces a shift in what the listener believes and does. By God's grace we preach for a change in people's lives! The central idea, therefore, has to have elements that make it worth remembering and repeating. That way, when your listeners are faced with a decision on Monday morning, they can remember the lesson of your central idea and put it into action.

How do we craft a memorable central idea? Here's a checklist for a central idea that will make a lasting impact on your listeners:

1. **Is it Singular?** *Have I identified ONE idea that I can develop throughout the sermon?*
2. **Is it Simple?** *Is the idea easy to express and to remember? According to one quote "Overstuffed equals under-explained". Matthew E. Mays, author of "The Laws of Subtraction", puts it this way: "Limiting information engages the imagination." Challenge yourself! Limit your central idea to 15 words.*
3. **Is it Stirring?** *Is the idea creative? Does it invoke an emotion? Is it intriguing? Does it inspire? Does it solve a problem that my congregation cares about? Have I given them a reason to want to remember this tomorrow or even make a remark about it today?*
4. **Is it Sticky?** *Even if the idea is worth remembering, is it worth repeating? Is it structured well? Does it evoke a response in you or in the congregation? Does it make anyone pay attention? If you're interested, go on YouTube and search for "The Catchy Song". The lyrics go something like this "This song's gonna get stuck inside your head..." (You can thank me later. Just email me your appreciation!). While I admit that the song can grow to be annoying, the concept is spot on. In order for an idea to take root and take over, it has to take hold of the recipient. This Word has to get stuck inside your head! The job of the preacher is to create a central idea that does just that. Now, just because your central idea is short, rhymes, or is based off of a popular song lyric or advertisement doesn't mean that the central idea will be remembered. If you are not careful, the congregation will walk away*

remembering the advertisement or the song you're referencing instead of your sermon! Do the hard work of sifting through the information to find a catchy central idea that will stick inside your listener's heads.

If you can say something memorable that both preacher and people care about in 15 words or less, you definitely have something meaningful to say! You have an idea that's ready to be preached! Congratulations!

I must admit, it feels wonderful to have a great idea. There's a sense of accomplishment that goes along with seeing an idea come to life. Remember, however, that while you have an idea, you do not have a sermon just yet. We still have some work to do before we develop and illustrate the idea in such a way that the listener is influenced by what we have to say...

That being said, let's keep working.

Step Five: Synchronize

The process of synchronization continues our mission to bring the sermon from "over there" to "over here". This is where we discover the rest of the content that helps further develop the central idea of the sermon. So far, we have the background information, word studies, observations, and answers to the questions we've asked. And although the sermon is beginning to take shape, it is still missing something. At this point, we are not only looking for details about the text that will make the sermon interesting, but we're also looking for details about the human experience that will make the sermon interesting to our people.

The synchronization process makes sure that we are not simply talking to the people about the Bible. It also ensures that we have more than just good advice about the human condition. The synchronization process helps us to responsibly apply the Bible to everyday life. We have taken the time to dig into the word of God. We're doing much more than producing a motivational speech with a Biblical text as a foundation. The synchronization step makes sure that the preacher doesn't go to either extreme. This is where we start looking for those details that are going to make the sermon both interesting and helpful. This is where we connect the cannon to the human condition and make sure that they can relate and understand. Why is this so important?

It is here that the preacher has to be careful. The "Curse of Knowledge" is described as finding it difficult to remember what it is like to not know something that we ourselves know well. To combat this curse, the preacher must be faithful in this part of the process so that he or she preaches a sermon that leaves the congregation saying, "This is what the Bible said to me!"

Now it's time to have a deeper conversation with the text. Here are some conversation starters that I use in an effort to synchronize for an interesting, impactful sermon:

1. *Is this an idea that my congregation (or this preacher) is passionate about?*
2. *Does this address something that is happening in the world, my community, or my church?*
3. *Does this idea address an upcoming event on the calendar?*
4. *Has this idea impacted me personally? How? Does it inspire me? Does it make me nervous?*
5. *Have I ever struggled with this concept?*
6. *How will this idea affect how my people's lives tomorrow?*
7. *How will they benefit from adopting this idea?*
8. *Who will get hurt if this text is misunderstood? How will they suffer?*
9. *How will someone from a different background receive this idea?*
10. *What are the reasonable objections to accepting this idea?*
11. *How does this idea challenge our norms?*
12. *What doesn't this idea teach that I expected?*
13. *Is this idea expressed anywhere else in the Bible?*
14. *If Jesus were here today, what would He say about my central idea?*
15. *What baggage am I bringing to the understanding of this idea?*

At this point, you may be questioning whether or not all of this is necessary. We have a text, we know what the Bible says, and we know what the Bible means. Don't we have enough to write the sermon? Not quite. The shaping process addresses the place where, according to Eugene Lowry, author of *The Homiletic Plot*, preachers are most deficient. Lowry found that the single greatest weakness of the average sermon is the weakness of diagnosis. Apparently, once we sift through the material and see the central idea, we rush towards setting up the sermon outline without giving ourselves the time and space to answer what could be the most important question in the process of preparation. The question of…Why?

This is why we continue to synchronize even after we sift. We seek for the sake of diagnosis and depth. The preacher who continues the process by "synchronization", has decided that the routine answers to routine questions about the text will not suffice. This preacher is mindful of the complexities of the human condition and has decided that God has something intelligent and insightful to add. Here the preacher is determined to bring the Bible and the lives of our brothers and sisters together.

This level of diagnosis rescues the congregation from the oversimplistic, dogmatic preaching that leaves them guilty and fosters fanaticism. They are not chastised from the pulpit because they are "bad". They are not criticized because they are "evil". Far from making excuses for or condoning sin, the preacher teaches the people that God understands the underlying causes, and His Word can address the underlying causes that prompt human beings to do what they do.

Why is this level of diagnosis in preaching so important? Listeners today live complicated lives. Often, the Bible is seen as disconnected and unable to deal with the complexities of our realities. Hence the need for synchronization. It is not that the Bible is somehow at fault. Rather this disconnect is the failure of the preacher! Sometimes preachers are in such a hurry to get people to do what we feel they are supposed to do, that we forget to tell people that God understands why people do the things that they do, and that God has not forgotten them. The God who created human beings is intimately familiar with the human condition. So much so, that when He wanted to express His love for us, He sent his "Word made flesh". Jesus Himself came and identified with every aspect of the human experience. Jesus showed that the Trinity understood what we go through and why we do what we do because Jesus lived it. His requests are not unreasonable, and His commands are not impossible. God knows us better than we know ourselves because of who Jesus is.

We do the Word of God a disservice if we neglect to seek more than just the usual applications and give more than just the customary answers. We must address today's problems. We must apply the Word to today's challenges. More than preaching with the Bible in one hand and the newspaper in the other, we must get past the surface and address why people react to the news the way they do and make the daily decisions that they make. We must go deeper.

God the Father is the greatest Communicator we have ever known. After all, His words have the power to do more than convey ideas. His words have the capacity to make those ideas come to life! When we first see God speaking in scripture, He is not only expressing what He would like to see happen, but simultaneously making things happen as He spoke. Being the infinitely effective communicator that He is, God could have limited His communication to either written or verbal form in an effort to convey His ideas to humankind. Yet God does more. He sends His Son, the "Word". Jesus, the ultimate form of communication. In a sense, when God wanted to connect with us and convey His love, He went as deep as He could possibly go. He sent Jesus. God's Son incarnate was the most well-rounded sermon our Heavenly Father could ever preach.

CHAPTER FIVE

WHEN A PLAN COMES TOGETHER

Step 6: Shaping

Give yourself a pat on the back. So far, you have a lot to work with. You have dug deep into the text. You went past the surface meanings, and you now have a lot of substance to add to the sermon. You have a great central idea, lots of details about the text, the background, and the original meaning. When it comes to the text you are studying, you have a lot to say. You also dug deep into the human condition and our applications are going way past the surface. You have taken the time to put some real thought into the motivations behind the behavior of the Biblical characters, and you have also spent time diagnosing your congregation. You are going to deal with more than just the "black and white". You are not prepared to wrestle with the gray areas of the text. This sermon will explore the complexities of the human condition. This sermon will deal with more than just what the Biblical characters did, but why they did it and the lessons we can learn.

What's more, all of this will be built on the solid foundation of the Biblical passage under consideration, which is most important. Not only will that idea be true to the scriptures, it will also be memorable and impactful. The idea will be singular, simple, sticky, and stirring. This will be an idea that the church will remember on Monday and share with their friends on Thursday. It will be a deciding factor in someone's decision-making this week. This sermon is going to make a difference in someone's life.

However, we can't stop now. It's almost time to preach.

Everything up to this point is an exercise in developing and clarifying ideas. We have spent the bulk of our preparation time trying to figure out what to say, and for good reason! Often, when we think of powerful sermons, what comes to mind is the display of charismatic delivery that we see behind the pulpit. In the heat of the sermonic moment, many preachers are enthralled with the dynamic nature of what the preacher did, never stopping to consider how he or she got the desired result. The effective sermon can be delivered powerfully, precisely because it was researched thoroughly and developed thoughtfully. In a sense, the effective sermon is an exercise in developing and clarifying an impactful, Biblical idea! It is when the preacher makes crafting this idea, clarifying this idea, and supporting this idea from the Bible the top priority, that powerful delivery becomes much easier to achieve.

We must also remember that having something to say does not absolve us from the responsibility of saying it well. The preacher's job is not only to research, but to relate. He or she must not only assemble the ingredients of this gourmet meal but prepare and present the delicacies in such a way that they are so appealing to those who would partake, that the congregation is left at the culmination of the experience wanting more. The preacher is responsible for both captivating content and dynamic delivery. If you are not responsible for this, then who is? You are the postal worker responsible for delivering the mail! We have to do everything in our power to make sure God's love letter reaches its intended destination. The first step towards effectively, authentically sharing your sermonic story in a way that will impact the minds of those who are listening, is to organize the material in the form that makes it comfortable for the preacher to deliver and comfortable for the congregation to receive. All of this begins with the outline.

The outline is a skeleton to which you will attach everything else that makes up the sermon. It will serve as a guide and help determine if you are faithfully expounding on the core idea. The outline will help the preacher be mindful of where he or she is taking the congregation and will help keep things clear for them so that both preacher and people arrive at the destination, known as the "conclusion", safe and sound. Even though most of the raw material we will be using has already been compiled, the outline is responsible for putting it all together. It serves as a "road map" for the sermon and, if the road map is not clear, then everything else that follows will automatically be cloudy, disjointed, and unclear. For the preacher and the listener, the outline is the difference between order and chaos. Order and clarity throughout the sermon preparation process is the ultimate goal.

Start a conversation about outlines and you're likely to never stop. There are as many ways to structure a sermon as there are topics to preach on. What's more, all of them can be effective. Every form has its advocates and benefits. Some preachers will tell you to save the main point for later in the sermon, while others will tell you that the main point needs to be stated up front. Many preachers believe every sermon should be told as a narrative because the Bible is, in a sense, one long story. Others are more comfortable with making classically organized logical arguments before the court of congregational opinion. Some preachers will remember their creative writing classes and advocate for an outline that has a clear introduction, thesis statement, and three points. Then there are those who skipped their Toastmasters meetings and believe instead that the preacher should travel through the text making as many observations as the passage and the people's attention spans allow. Not only can all of these methods prove to be effective to some extent, but they probably all need to be used at some point along the way. Why deliver the sermon the same way all the time? There's no need to predictably follow one form simply because that form is the "best". Even your favorite food can get boring if it's prepared and served in the same way every time. Change is good!

Whatever form you decide to use, there are six characteristics that every outline must have if the sermon is going to be successful. Those six characteristics are going to be present in Preach E.A.S.Y. so it's best that I introduce them now.

Every sermon outline should be:

1. *Clear*
2. *Cohesive*
3. *Concise*
4. *Centered*
5. *Creative*
6. *Connecting*

Let's take some time to discuss why each of these is so important.

Clarity

If nothing else, when I'm taking a trip, I want my directions to be clear. There's nothing more anxiety inducing than coming to a fork in the road and not being able to decide whether to go right or left because the directions aren't clear about where to go next. Confusing directions have left many a traveler frustrated. Confusing, meandering sermons are no different. No matter how you choose to arrange your content, clarity should be job number one.

As the old saying goes, "A mist in the pulpit is a fog in the pew". The abundance of foggy pews is a testament to the fact that the hard work of thinking until the preacher is absolutely clear about what needs to be said, is not being done. Thinking is hard work and thinking deeply is even more difficult. Thinking clearly? Now, that's another level of dedication altogether. If your outline doesn't have a clear, logical progression or if it needs to be explained, then you still have work to do in order to clarify. The outline for an effective sermon should be so clear that, if someone were to take your outline just before you stood up to preach, they would be able to preach your sermon from start to finish without any assistance from you. The expositions (points of the sermon) should be Biblical, the progressions logical, the applications practical, and the illustrations useful. Everything should fit. Everything about your sermon should be clear.

Cohesiveness

Along with clarity, every sermon outline should strive for cohesiveness. Not only does everything the preacher says need to be related to the text that is being preached, but the points being made, the illustrations of those points, and the applications should all relate to each other. At no point during the journey should the listener ever have to ask: "Now, where are we again?" Every aspect of the sermon should be crystal clear and fit so well that the listener should be able to follow you without additional explanation. If the illustration needs further illustrating, it probably doesn't belong. If the explanation needs further explanation, then there is more work to be done. Anyone who is traveling will avoid unnecessary detours, especially if they have somewhere they need to be. Some trips are longer than others, and some may even involve a few additional turns. However, no one wants to drive around the block for no reason, especially when they want to go home! Tangents in a sermon waste time and can serve to distract and discourage a listener who just wants the preacher to get to the point so they can go home! If you're going to preach an effective sermon, make sure everything fits.

Concision

"If I had more time, I would have written a shorter letter."

The truth is, if most preachers invested more time, energy, and focus they would write much shorter (and better) sermons. The shortest distance between two points is a straight line, yet many sermons insist on going "over the river and through the woods" in order to get to the point. If your preaching is going to improve, it has to get more concise. Time has become more precious than ever, with attention spans shortening every day. The sermon has to take that into consideration. Granted, I hear the rebuttals all the time. "If you can sit through a movie for two hours, then you should be able to give Jesus an hour of your time." I have news for you: You are neither Luke Skywalker, nor are you Iron Man. If you were, you'd have a case for being long-winded. Especially when you are saving the world! Unfortunately, you are not (unless you are, in which case, your sermon illustrations are going to be AMAZING!). Now that we've gotten that out of the way, let's talk some more about being concise.

If you remember the Microsoft study that highlighted our goldfish sized attention spans, then you realize why shorter presentations make sense. It's not that people don't want to sit and listen to you. Nowadays, they just can't. We are not wired for the extended discourses of yesteryear. It's time for us to let them go. Nowadays a caption can convey an entire thought in less than a paragraph. TED speakers spread ideas that change the world in less than 18 minutes. Surely the move of God you intended for this service can be achieved in less than 90 minutes. While God is not bound by time, the attention span of the average human being is, and we are not communicating effectively if no one is paying attention to what we have to say!

Admittedly, stories can help to expand the capacity for attention and retention. Stories, analogies, metaphors and similes can also help in expressing complicated concepts in a clear and concise way. Use stories as much as possible (more on that in a bit) but remember that not even the best storytelling can keep the interest of a listener who has run out of patience, or help a sermon that has run out of time. In order to preach effectively, the preacher has to try his or her best to shorten the sermon to the point where those who are listening can digest and appreciate what is being shared.

Here's a side note: According to the dictionary, the word "conciseness" is just as acceptable as the word "concision". However, I chose concision because, well… that word just happens to be more concise! When in doubt, get to the point! Your listeners will rarely be disappointed.

Centering

There's a saying that goes, "To a hammer, everything looks like a nail". There's so much material to cover on any given subject, that sometimes the temptation to make something fit is almost irresistible. This is especially true when it comes to the things that preachers are most passionate about. There are "hammers" in pulpits everywhere who just can't help but see nails in every text they read, every time they preach. Biblical preaching allows for variety. Without the Biblical context as our guide, every application is the same and every sermon sounds identical. Sermons that are rooted in scripture help the preacher avoid agendas and hobby horses. Biblical preaching also allows the preacher to be grounded in truth. Why say something that the Bible does not say?

Centered preaching steers clear of false hopes based on false teaching. We don't make promises that God never intended to keep, by saying things that God never intended His Word to say. How can we in good conscience avoid saying something that the Bible clearly says? Centered preaching treats sin the same way God does. It provides guidance for those in the culture who are trying to live like Christ by pointing them to Biblical principles, even if those principles are difficult. Preaching that is centered in scripture avoids heresy by remaining grounded in Biblical truth.

Centered preaching also promotes Biblical literacy. If a study were conducted, I believe many preachers would be surprised as to how unfamiliar their congregations are with the Bible. Of course, everyone has a favorite passage of scripture. Many even quote or reference the Bible for whatever reason. Few, however, are familiar with what the Bible actually has to say, especially when it comes to the issues about which they have already made up their minds. Centered preaching brings to mind those portions of the Bible our people may have forgotten or neglected to study. They also help the preacher expand his or her area of study. Pet sermons and pet subjects often come from pet passages of scripture. Preaching centered in the Bible will eventually draw us into unfamiliar territory and force us to flex our investigative muscles to discover what else the Bible has to say.

Creativity

For many preachers, this is the last item on the list. After all, if the sermon outline is centered, cohesive, concise, and clear, then what else is there to accomplish? Admittedly, the tools I just mentioned are enough to enable any preacher to preach a good sermon. Here is an additional step for those who want to further elevate their preaching from good to great. There is a 24 hour-a-day competition for our attention. Social media ads, television ads, print ads and others are constantly screaming, "look at me", as we go throughout our day. The assumption that the preacher is automatically granted the attention of those in attendance because they're in church and a sermon is being preached, is wishful thinking. It's not enough for the content to be correct, it must also be creative. This is going to require time and thought, but the results are definitely worth the work.

Connecting

"What does this have to do with me?" The preacher can be certain that this question will be on the minds of their congregations every time they rise to preach. We live in a culture that is, for the most part, disconnected from the history and the life of the church, and often sees the church as an irrelevant relic of yesteryear. With the challenges of everyday living becoming more formidable every day, people are now looking to the church and the Bible for more than just the story of Jesus. To paraphrase John F. Kennedy, the sentiment nowadays seems to be, "Ask not what you can do for your Savior. Ask what your Savior can do for you!" The preacher would not be a faithful messenger if he or she did nothing but indulge societal selfishness. That being said, there has to be some connection between what is said from the pulpit and what is experienced at the office all week long.

Those who believe in the authority of scripture also believe that the Bible addresses every aspect of our lives. If that is the case, then the Bible must have something to say about how we are treated and how we treat each other. The Bible must have something to say about how we spend our money and how we raise our children. The Bible must also have something to say about how we treat our neighbors, employees, the underprivileged, minorities, enemies, family and friends. The message of the Bible must connect to every aspect of our lives and it is the responsibility of the preacher to ensure that the message makes that connection. Granted, God is not going to re-write the Scriptures for our comfort. We cannot change the Bible. It was designed to change us. However, when we preach in a way that connects, it DOES change us. It makes a major difference in our lives.

Not only must we preach a message that connects, but the sermon must be preached in a way that connects. The eloquent oration of the past is quickly losing its impact, as it gives way to a more casual style of speaking that focuses on authenticity and connection with the listener. Cathy Heller, author and host of the podcast "Don't Keep Your Day Job" is fond of saying, "Casual is the new formal", and society is proving that she's correct. The manicured phrases formerly used to impress congregations with our intelligence are now only impressive in academic circles. And even in those circles, erudition is losing its luster. There's a basic sales principle that says, "People buy from people they know, like, and trust". Stories and simple language help people feel that they know, like and trust you. In order to be an effective preacher, you have to connect.

Here is a simple, straightforward format that helps both the preacher and the people. You will find that it helps you effectively, authentically share your story. Here's the 8-step outline I have designed:

1. *Connect through a story*
2. *Connect to their story*
3. *Connect to the Bible story*
4. *State the central theme*
5. *Ask the central question*
6. *Have a conversation*
7. *Come to a climax*
8. *Call the congregation to action*

Here's how this format looks in a sermon:

Connect Through A Story

The responsibility of the introduction is to connect. The preacher should begin the sermon in a way that grabs the listeners' attention and there are four main ways he or she can use to accomplish this. The preacher can use a statistic, a quote, a question or a story. While each of these is effective in their own right, I believe that the most effective way to connect is through a story. What do I mean by a story? According to

Annette Simmons, author of the book "The Story Factor": "Basically, a story is a narrative account of an event or events-true or fictional." Most who study stories agree that metaphor, analogy, and narrative can all be considered when we mention "story", and the preacher uses one of these to invite the audience to begin the sermonic journey. Stories work because they get people's attention, peak their interest, and connect them to the rest of the sermon.

A story also helps to build the trust necessary for the listeners to allow themselves to be persuaded by your material and before you attempt to influence anyone, you need to establish enough trust to successfully deliver your message. As a matter of fact, the confidence people have in who you are can be a conduit for the rest of your message. That makes stories extremely important!

The human brain is wired to respond to stories more effectively than a presentation of logical information. While the brain can process and does appreciate linear thought, even a story that is badly told will do more to grab the audience than a bland discussion of the facts. A good story simplifies those facts and turns them into something that can be easily understood. Then it makes those facts memorable. People tune in to stories. People remember stories. People relate to stories. People trust storytellers. People are persuaded by stories. People pay attention to stories. There really isn't a more effective method of communication in existence when it comes to conveying information and changing minds. Simply put, if your goal is to preach for changed lives, then you should want the congregation to be interested and invested in you and in what is being said. Stories accomplish that effectively.

They should be used liberally throughout, but at the very least you should start your sermon with a story.

To be clear, a story doesn't have to begin with "Once upon a time" and end with "And they lived happily ever after". As a matter of fact, any shared life experiences would be effective in grabbing the congregation's attention. And as far as explaining is concerned, a simple comparison (The Kingdom of God is like a mustard seed) will accomplish much more in less time. A preacher can use any style of story in an effort to connect the congregation to the sermon. Here are some examples of the types of shared life experiences (stories) any preacher can use:

Stories About Nature
Stories about nature are among the most time-honored and universally understood stories a preacher can tell. Jesus told these stories (A sower went forth to sow...) and they have stood the test of time.

Personal Life Experiences
Without making yourself the hero of every sermon, sharing a personal life experience can help the congregation to connect with the speaker and the sermon. These can also be the easiest to access and remember. They can also be the most effective stories to tell because of your familiarity with the details.

A Story From History
Historical figures and events hold lessons for us if we allow ourselves to be taught. Searching the pages of history for the perfect anecdote can be tedious at times, but these are well worth the effort. Church history, background stories about hymns and popular songs, and little-known historical facts can also serve to introduce the sermon.

A Story About The Passage
Sometimes the background information about why the passage was written, where it was written, and the author can serve to connect the sermon with the congregation. Even details about the passage itself, it's relation to the rest of the chapter, or the rest of the Bible can be helpful. For example, Mark often uses the word "immediately" to describe Jesus' movements, yet Jesus takes a blind man outside of the city in Mark chapter 8 and subjects Him to a process. Just a description of the story behind the text can shed some light on what the congregation is being shown.

Certainly, there are other means of introducing the sermon. Quotes, questions and statistics are among the most effective. That being said, stories are among the easiest to remember for both the preacher and the people, and they are almost guaranteed to accomplish the goal of getting people's attention. I have never heard a speaker go wrong when they started with the right story.

Connect To Their Story
The preacher can and probably should begin with a story, but they certainly can't stay there. As a matter of fact, the story becomes a

distraction if it isn't quickly connected to the people. You are telling this story, but what does it have to do with me? Why are you telling me this story? Why are you preaching this sermon? Why should I listen? What does any of this have to do with me? After you've started with a story, quickly continue by talking about the experiences of people in the pews and why this subject is important to them.

For example: "Just like the tortoise lacked physical speed in his contest against the hare, so we often lack the physical resources and abilities required to conquer life's challenges."

Now you have invited the congregation to continue along on the journey. By making the content personally relevant, you have demanded my attention and given yourself the opportunity to move towards the meat of the message.

Connect To The Bible Story

Finally, we are connected. You grabbed my attention by telling me a story, and now you're talking about me and relating to my personal story. But this is more than a motivational talk, this is a sermon, and sermons are fundamentally based on the Bible. So, what exactly does any of this have to do with the Bible? This is the part of the sermon where you make sure that question is answered. Once we have connected with the people, the speaker must now move to connect the people with the Word. For example:

> "Just like Dory in the movie "Finding Nemo" encourages Nemo to keep on swimming. The woman with an issue of blood encourages us to keep on pressing. Hers is a lesson we all need to learn."

Notice how the sermon begins to transition from the general to the specific. With the congregation's attention in tow, we now build the case for the sermon to come. So far, the introduction has pulled the ancient text and the present congregation closer together, making the presentation more relevant and interesting. The introduction has served its purpose: to develop the argument, arouse interest in the subject, and build a bridge to the congregation.

State The Central Theme

The central theme is the backbone of the sermon. It determines the direction that the body of the sermon will take and provides the underlying question that the body will answer. This is the main idea that the sermon will expand. The central theme serves as a contract of sorts, ensuring that the preacher does not go off on a tangent. Every point that is made, every illustration that is added, every explanation given, and every application included will be related to the core of the sermon. The introduction will lead into the central theme, the conclusion will celebrate the central theme, and the call to action will invite the congregation to do something in response to how the central theme has challenged them. Once the preacher has connected with the congregation and continued to develop his or her argument throughout the remainder of the introduction, the next step is to introduce the central theme which will guide the rest of the outline.

Ask The Central Question
The central theme will serve as the basis for the central question. This leads directly to the body of the sermon and dictates what will be preached. The conversation to follow is a direct answer to the central question which is derived from the central theme. For example:

"The storm that strikes while Jesus is in the boat with his disciples teaches them lessons about the character of their Lord (Central theme). What lessons does the storm teach the disciples about the Savior? (Central question)

As you can see, the central question frames the discussion to follow and makes sure that everything will be streamlined and easy to digest throughout the remainder of the sermon. Now for the main event.

Have A Conversation
The next step in our sermonic journey (which also happens to be the longest and most detailed step) is the conversation. This is the body of the sermon where the central theme is explained, illustrated, and applied. For many preachers, the conversation consists of three points, while others extract as many points as they think are reasonable from the text. Studies show that people effectively remember data in sets of three, which is why three points are usually recommended. That being said, the preacher should neither spend time searching for a third point that does not exist, nor ignore a fourth or fifth point that clearly comes from the text. Three points are good, but three alliterated points are even better in that they allow the outline to appear more organized

and easier to remember. The preacher is permitted, however, to make as many points as necessary in order to complete the task of supporting the central theme.

Each point of the conversation, or "moves", according to H. Grady Davis in his classic, "Design for Preaching", should consist of three components:

1. *Explanations*
2. *Illustrations*
3. *Applications*

Each of these elements contributes toward and is necessary to the goal of an effective, authentic sermon. They all work together to accomplish the purpose of understanding. In the interest of clarity, here's another look at how each point should be structured:

1. *Say it*
2. *Show it*
3. *Make it stick*

Let's take a moment to discuss what each should accomplish and how each should fit:

Explanations: Say It

Most textbooks on preaching would refer to this as "exposition", and its importance cannot be overstated. Here we are referring to the portion of the conversation where we make reference to and explain what the Bible is saying. According to Chris Anderson, "A major finding of cognitive psychology is that long-term memory depends on coherent hierarchical organization of content." (TED Talks, p. 79) That is to say, each point should come from the text and should connect with the other points in such a way that it shows a logical progression from beginning to end. I came across a post where another TED speaker, puts it this way:

> "A talk is not a container or a bin that you can put content in, it is a process. A trajectory. The goal is to take the listener from where he is to someplace new."

Each point, or explanation, comes from the text under consideration and moves us through the progression of thought from where we started at the beginning of the sermon, to some new understanding about the passage we are considering from the Bible. The goal is for each point to come so directly from the Bible that the listener can follow along without much leading. Then, while each point is being clearly explained from scripture, the preacher uses the information gained from "sifting" and "synchronizing" to ensure that each point goes beyond a surface interpretation of scripture or a shallow understanding of life. The explanation will include observations about the text based on the word study, background, and research questions that will help make the Bible clear.

And how are these points being expressed so that they are clear? Research into the world of advertising offers some help here. Studies suggest that short, provocative, repeatable phrases are more likely to be retweeted, posted on Facebook and repeated in the news cycle.

In the land of social media, the soundbite is the king.

Most ad campaigns have recognizable slogans that are designed to bring the company to mind when you hear them. In songwriting, the "hook" is often the focus of the song, because that is the portion that is more portable and brings the song to mind when you hear it. These expositions, according to the experts, should be stated in the form of sticky soundbites (or hooks, if you prefer), which allow the main points of the sermon to be more easily repeated and remembered. When the points from your sermon stick, the rest of the message comes to mind when you hear them.

For example:

> "Here we see that the King has signed a law that attacks Daniel's ability to pray. The enemy could have attacked Daniel in any other way, but He chose Daniel's source of spiritual connection. Why?

"Everything is affected when you and I are not connected."

Illustrations: Show It

Each point made during the conversation is like a mile marker along the road in our journey. These help us take note of how far along the journey we are and whether or not we are headed toward the destination of our conclusion. The landscape would be barren, and the journey would be boring without landmarks and sights that make things interesting, comprehensible, and memorable. These are your illustrations, and no sermon is effective without them. Here's another way of communicating the importance of stories: Without a story, facts don't mean anything.

You can try to take the congregation on a journey without providing the scenery of illustrations, and you will have bored, disconnected people on your hands. Stories make the trip more enjoyable and more memorable.

Illustrations are an important part of every sermon. Whether as stories or comparisons, illustrations help us understand, remember the content of the conversation, and make things clearer. Providing facts without stories leaves too much to chance. Using stories to illustrate, helps people remember and more fully understand the sermon. While there is a constant fear of stories being used too often or used inappropriately or ineffectively, the general consensus is that including illustrations in an effort to describe instead of explain, can always do more good, than harm.

Once again, stories don't have to be long, detailed, or follow the traditional format that we're used to, but they must be included. Giving people facts as a method of influence can be a waste of time. When you give a story along with the facts, you stand a better chance of influencing others with the message by encouraging them to share your interpretation. So, where do we get these illustrations? This is yet another area where our S.P.O.T.E.R. comes in handy. During our study, observation, thinking or exposure, we are likely to find illustrative material that we can use to bring our sermon to life. While it isn't mandatory to have each point followed by an illustration, most effective preaching does just as much or more illustrating as it does explaining, in an effort to make sure that the lessons being taught actually take hold. Try adding one illustration to each point in the sermon and watch the sermon become more memorable and impactful in the minds of those who are listening. Show more than you say.

While we are adding illustrations, there is cause for concern and caution. Here are a few areas where the responsible preacher should be on the lookout for the dangers of misusing illustrations:

The preacher can rely too heavily on illustrations and spend little to no time explaining or applying the Word. Illustrations are helpful and necessary, but there is such a thing as too many. Use just enough illustrations to paint a picture of the idea you are trying to explain, and then move on to the next idea. Stacking stories for the sake of telling them can be entertaining, but the stories can also serve as a distraction, which takes away from the overall focus and power of the sermon.

Illustrations can also be used in lieu of explanations, which defeats the purpose of using the illustrations altogether. Remember, in order for an illustration to be effective, there must be something to illustrate. Without the substance of explanation, the illustrations are simply entertaining stories placed throughout the body of the sermon to pass the time. Use the Biblically grounded explanation to state your case. The illustrations show more clearly what you have already stated. Put them together and every point in the sermon is both stated and shown for maximum impact.

Illustrations can be well used and well placed, but they can also be too long. Too much unnecessary detail can leave the congregation lost within the stories and unable or unwilling to follow you further.

An illustration that doesn't illustrate, is a distraction that the preacher cannot afford. If the illustration you are using doesn't make your point clearer, but requires further clarification, then the illustration either needs help or needs to be replaced. The illustration should teach the lesson of the text with such clarity that the congregation takes away the lesson and keeps it permanently.

Applications: Make It Stick

The application of each point is the final bridge between passage and people. This is where, with the help of the explanation and the illustrations, the preacher answers the question: "What does this mean to me." This is where the Word of God comes and moves into my neighborhood. This is where the Bible is allowed to influence my decision making and impact my life. What do I do with the text at home? How do I live the principles of this passage on my job? What are the benefits of these lessons as I am preaching to my family? How does this impact my choice of recreation? Does this have anything to do with the conflict I need to resolve or the people in my life I need to forgive? Where am I being challenged? What areas of my life need to be changed? What does this have to do with the people around me and the society in which I live?

There are some schools of thought that believe that applications only serve to rob the Bible of its ability to speak for itself. I beg to differ. Nehemiah 8:8 (NIV) records a scene in which the Levites read God's law to the waiting congregation. In an effort to provide responsible instruction, they "read from the Book of the Law of God, making it clear and giving the meaning so that the people understood what was being read." Scripture was not left up to individual interpretation, but explanation and applications were given so that those who were in attendance would understand. Furthermore, it was Jesus' application of His sermon about the Good Samaritan in Luke 10 that gives us all something to think about. The Bible reads, "So which one of these three do you think was neighbor to him who fell among the thieves? Go, and do likewise." (Luke 10:36-37 NKJV). Here, Jesus not only makes his point with an explanation, "Do this and you will live" (Luke 10: 28) but also goes further by using an illustration (the story of the Good Samaritan). He then concludes by not allowing the questioning lawyer to draw his own conclusions, but rather driving the point home with an application that is impossible to escape. The effective, authentic sermon will apply the Word to people's lives so that those who are hearing are clear to what the Bible is teaching as God's will for them.

Conclusion

As the saying goes, "All good things must come to an end". Ask any listener, and they will tell you that no matter how interesting the presentation, the sermon is definitely one of those things. But, how exactly do we bring the sermon to a comfortable close?

We can't just…stop. The effective sermon misses an opportunity to make a maximum impact when it fizzles out. After being invited on the journey via the connection, taken through the continuation with the central theme, and engaged in the conversation, we owe it to our congregations to not just kick them out of the vehicle and let them fend for themselves the rest of the way. The preacher proposed that the congregation take a journey and then presented them with a destination. For the sake of closure, every beginning should have an ending. It is the responsibility of the preacher to ensure that we all arrive at the end of the sermon. This means that a conclusion is in order.

As any member of any church anywhere will tell you, the sermon should eventually end. How the sermon closes, however, is another matter. While there are different ideas on how to conclude the sermon, the most effective preachers show us that no impactful sermon should end without a celebration of the gospel. Not only should the body of the sermon feature an in-depth conversation about the central theme, but the conclusion should celebrate the good news of that theme. Why should we be glad to hear this? Why should we take this home? Decision-making is impacted by celebration, as celebration activates emotion and people are more likely to remember events that made them feel good.

In addition to the emotional activation involved in celebration, there is another component. The "serial position effect" is the tendency of a person to recall the first and last items in a series most accurately. If we pair these two facts together, we learn that people tend to remember things that make them feel good, and people tend to remember things that come either first or last, then we discover that the introduction and the conclusion of the sermon are of the utmost importance. The conclusion has the potential to be the most memorable part of the sermon. This is an opportunity that the preacher cannot afford to waste!

So exactly how do we make the most of our conclusions? Here are some guidelines:

Quit When You're Done

One of the most discouraging mistakes a preacher can make is the refusal to stop preaching even when he or she has no sermon left to preach. When you've come to the end of your sermon, stop talking. It's that simple. Once the central theme has been discussed and all the points in your sermon have been explained, illustrated and applied, the responsible, effective preacher takes it upon his or herself to bring the sermon to a close. This is not the time to introduce new information, clarify unclear explanations, tell additional stories, or include "one more thing". Once the sermon has come to a close, it is time for the preacher to come to the conclusion and let God's people go.

The Conclusion Is Celebration Time!

The conclusion of the sermon has the potential to be one of the most memorable portions of the entire experience. The genius of black preaching is that this genre not only uses the serial position effect to its advantage (making sure that the end of the sermon is impactful so as to render the entire sermon more memorable), but black preaching also includes celebration. This is effective because according to psychology, we are more likely to remember events that arouse our emotions than events that elicit a neutral response. Celebrations are memorable by nature, which is why preachers cannot afford to miss the opportunity to make a lasting impact on the congregation. We must celebrate the gospel!

Rebecca Todd, a University of Toronto professor, discovered that, how vividly a person experiences an event influences how easily he or she can recall the event or the information connected with the event later on. Marketing professionals understand this all too well, which is why they spend millions of dollars each year making sure that they create ads that force their viewers to feel. The sermon should also make the listener feel, and the conclusion is the most obvious, natural, and impactful way to accomplish this.

Please note that celebration has more to do with content than with style. Frank Thomas, author of the book "They Like to Never Quit Praising God" defined celebration as, "The culmination of sermonic design, where a moment is created in which the remembrance of a redemptive past and/or the conviction of a liberated future transforms the events immediately experienced." This definition mentions nothing about volume or intonation. Rather, the focus is on the good news that was preached in the text being highlighted and applied to people in a way they can relate using language they can understand.

In light of this definition, no preacher should shy away from the concept of celebrating the gospel present in the passage because of their denomination, race or culture. While every culture may celebrate the good news in its own way, every culture and every congregation should recognize and celebrate the good news! No matter what your background, Calvary is still powerful. The blood of Jesus still cleanses regardless of what language you speak. God promises deliverance for His people no matter your preferred style of worship. Recognize and highlight the good news in the text and you will leave a permanent, undeniable impression on those who are gathered to hear you preach.

CHAPTER SIX
HIS STORY, YOUR STORY

Step 7: Say It

In the book of Romans, Paul remarks that, "Faith cometh by hearing, and hearing by the Word of God." (Romans 10:17) And while advances in technology have afforded us many different means of sharing the gospel and changes in the culture have demanded an evolution in how we preach the gospel, there is still something unique and divinely ordained about hearing the Word of God. This is the method by which God has decided that human beings come to an understanding of Jesus. Here, the Apostle Paul says, "For after that in the wisdom of God the world by wisdom knew not God, it pleased God by the foolishness of preaching to save them that believe." (1 Cor. 1:21) If people are going to be saved, a person has to preach. Which brings us to the final stages of our process. The preparations are completed; the research is over. The outline has been written and everything is in place. The weekend is almost here. You are ready to preach! Or are you...

You're almost ready, but not quite. Most preachers would consider themselves adequately prepared, but not you. Not yet. As an effective, authentic preacher seeking to share your story, you realize that there's one very important element still missing from the sermon. To master this last step will make the difference between a mediocre and an effective sermon. This last step will leave your congregation completely convinced that they have heard from Jesus. This final step makes all the difference.

The Sermon Has To Become YOUR Story

More than just a well thought out, well researched, and well-crafted presentation, the sermon has to become yours. The preacher can't just deliver it. The preacher has to OWN it. The Bible is God's story given to human beings, but the sermon must become our story about what God has to say. Philip Brooks famously defined preaching as, "Truth through personality." We've repeated that definition so many times that we've managed to miss the meaning.

If preaching was truth without personality, we would call it research. There is definitely a place for research because research is truth. We need to be educated. We need to be informed. We need truth, for according to scripture, it is truth that "sets us free". Truth is important but preaching must be more.

If preaching was truth through someone else's personality, we would call it acting. There's definitely a place in our society for acting. The ability of talented people to accurately portray different characters has come to play an important part in helping to shape the way we understand and see the world. From entertainment to marketing, actors and actresses are invaluable. However, preaching is not a portrayal of a personality, it is truth through personality. It is not enough to echo someone else's personality. Preaching must be more.

Preaching has been popularly defined as truth through personality. Whose personality? YOUR personality! The preacher has a personal experience with the text, and then he or she draws upon what God has given them to share about the gospel they have experienced. The preacher studies, prays, prepares, internalizes, and preaches the message, all while personalizing the presentation. To be sure, the sermon is not about you, but it does emanate from you. You are effectively, authentically, sharing your story.

Making the story yours involves comfort. Comfort is the goal for both you and your congregation. Comfort reduces distractions, makes reception and retention easier, and makes the overall preaching experience more enjoyable and more memorable. Comfort does not automatically mean that what you are saying has to make everyone feel comfortable all of the time. Even if the message you are delivering is difficult, listening to and remembering that message should not be. From the time you approach the pulpit until the time you end the sermon and sit down, you as the preacher are responsible for ensuring the comfort of everyone under your influence that day.

You Should Be Comfortable With You!

I was in a conversation one day, and for some odd reason I couldn't keep still. I kept fidgeting and looking around as if I was in some kind of danger. The person I was talking to noticed and brought it to my attention. "You're making me nervous", he said, and we all know where he was coming from. From the time the preacher approaches the people, he or she gives verbal and nonverbal indications of how comfortable they are with the moment and the task at hand. While some preachers downplay their introductions, it is worth noting that even the biographical information shared in those moments before you preach can go a long way towards giving the impression that it is safe to listen to you because you can handle it.

Gone are the days when the congregation will give you their attention simply because you stand behind the pulpit with a Bible in your hand and purport to preach the truth. Time is now more precious than ever, and there is constant competition for your congregation's attention. The confidence you have as a speaker (or lack thereof) will help to focus the congregation, win you a few moments of good will which you can use to begin your sermon, and set the tone for the rest of your time in the pulpit. Are you sure that this is what God wants you to say? Are you comfortable with the work you've put in? Are you excited about the message? Would you rather be doing something else? The confidence you convey will send an initial signal to the congregation. They will take their cues from you.

You Should Be Comfortable With Your Material

I spend a significant amount of time traveling. When I travel, I sometimes have to ask for directions. I've noticed that I can tell almost instantly how well someone knows the way just by how they share their information. Not only are they sure about what comes next, but they can share the necessary details, alternate routes, and tailor the material to be as detailed or as brief as the situation demands. This is the level of mastery that makes us comfortable. Consider this: If you aren't sure about the material, then why should I trust you to share it with me? How are you beginning the sermon? Have you mastered your introduction? How are you ending the sermon? Have you memorized your conclusion? Are you comfortable with the points being made throughout the sermon? Can you remember them? Are they crafted in such a way that your congregation can remember them? Can you transition from point to point comfortably? Have you mastered the material well enough to be able to adjust for time? Can you say more about each point if you had to? Can you say less? Can you share the illustrations, or will you forget the details of the story if you don't read them? Effective delivery has everything to do with how comfortable the preacher is with the material. Standup comedians do an excellent job of internalizing large chunks of material for their performances. Lawyers who deliver effective opening and closing arguments often have to do the same. Here are some tips that both professions use to get comfortable:

1. **Internalize your introduction.** *Word for word memorization can leave room for mishaps. What happens if you forget? Nothing is more embarrassing than a preacher who memorized a script but is fumbling over the lines. Internalize the material until it becomes your own. This is YOUR story! The introduction should be so familiar that you can preach it different ways, even while distracted. That way, no matter how much pressure accompanies the preaching moment, the preacher will always be able to stand and deliver with confidence.*
2. **Internalize the conclusion.** *There should be no guessing game as to how you are going to end. As discussed earlier, the sermon most effectively ends when the message culminates in a recognition of the good news of the text which results in a celebration of the gospel. The question the preacher must answer is, "How exactly are we going to celebrate?" Reverting to a familiar story, mindless repetition, or abruptly ending the sermon do not celebrate the gospel. Neither does the announcement "in conclusion", followed by a recapitulation of what was previously said. Take the time to discover the good news of the text and then select a story that illustrates the good news and leave that with the people. Your conclusion will be memorable, and the congregation will be thankful.*
3. **Memorize your points.** *Memorizing the points in the sermon will allow both you and your congregation to be comfortable with the progression and presentation of the message. I suggest verbatim memorization here because the goal is to deliver these points in exactly the way you want them to be remembered and repeated. This goal of memorization is one of the reasons why effective preachers traditionally stick with three points. People remember things in groups of three. There are many ways in which you can craft your points to help yourself and your congregation remember.*

Some preachers use alliteration. (Repetition of the same letter at the beginning of successive words). For example: Alliteration attracts and arrests attention. The points of the sermon can be alliterated which can make them easier to take away. The points of a sermon on compassion could be alliterated this way:

1. *Remember your humanity*
2. *Recognize our connection*
3. *Restore the fallen*

Another useful rhetorical device is anaphora (repetition of the same word or words at the beginning of successive phrases, clauses, or sentences). Much like alliteration, the beginning is repeated in order to help the speaker and listener remember. Using anaphora to organize your points in a sermon about Christ's sacrifice might look like this:

1. *He took our pain.*
2. *He took our problems.*
3. *He took our place.*

A third rhetorical device often used is epiphora (also called epistrophe- repetition of the same word or words at the end of two or more successive clauses, phrases or sentences). This is another way of organizing your material so that both you and the congregation are comfortable with what is being shared. A sermon on Romans 8 "If God be for us", might be outlined like this:

1. *Our enemies are against us.*
2. *Our efforts could not save us.*
3. *God is for us.*
4. *No one can conquer us.*

Notice that four points are used instead of three. Three points can make the sermon more memorable, but they are not mandatory. Using these rhetorical devices can also help achieve that goal.

No matter how you choose to craft your points, make them concise and creative so that they stick in your mind and in the mind of your listeners. Utilize various literary devices and give yourself the time to do what is necessary to memorize these guidelines before you preach.

Be familiar with your illustrations. If you are not going to use illustrations that have happened to you, you must be able to tell the story as if it happened to you. Stories provide amazing opportunities to give the congregation insight into the message, but they can't look deeper into the text if they are distracted by your poor telling of the story. Be familiar with the story and how you plan to apply it, or don't tell the story at all.

Writing out a full manuscript is another important step that helps the preacher and the congregation become more comfortable with the delivery of the sermon. A manuscript helps the preacher become more comfortable by helping to crystalize the thoughts on paper and bring clarity to his or her thinking. It is easier to review and edit a document you can see, and as any writer knows, editing is a necessity. Ernest Hemmingway is quoted as saying, "The first draft of anything is .... "(Look up the quote. I promise you won't be disappointed). The question that remains then is: how can we preach sermons from the pulpit that have not been first drafted in the study? Many congregations get the unedited comments about the text from preachers who think it's too time-consuming or inconvenient to write out their sermons.

To be clear, I am not advocating for manuscript preaching. I believe that comfort is the goal, not precision. If you are comfortable preaching from an outline and you have mastered the introduction, conclusion, points and illustrations, then by all means, preach from an outline. If you are comfortable preaching without notes and you know what you're going to say and how you're going to move through the sermon without rambling, then by all means, preach without notes. However, if you decide to preach, please take the time to write out, word for word, what you will be saying so that you can be absolutely sure.

If you were called upon to give remarks at the next Royal wedding, you would not think twice about taking every step possible to ensure that your material was clear, and that you were clear on your material. Why? You value the engagement of course! The venue is important. The attendees are important. You can't afford to mess this up, and those responsible for the invitation would be terribly disappointed if you did. This engagement matters and every person participating would treat it as if it matters. I hope and pray that you realize that the congregation you will address also matters. The King of heaven valued them enough to send Jesus Christ to die for their sins. Therefore, this engagement is important. These attendees are important. We cannot afford to mess this up. The One responsible for the invitation to preach would be disappointed if we did. So yes, the rhetorical devices may seem unnecessary, but organization matters. Memorization and internalization might seem inconvenient, but your familiarity with the material matters. Writing a manuscript seems like unnecessary work, but the preparation matters. This is all important because we are doing this for the people and to the glory of God.

This equals effective preaching! So how do we get comfortable enough to deliver effective sermons?

You should not make your congregation uncomfortable with the preaching experience.

Isaiah 20:2 records God's command to the prophet Isaiah to walk around naked and barefoot. This was designed to get his congregation's attention and no doubt, it made people uncomfortable. It is a stunning example of the preacher's obedience to the command of God even though that command was inconvenient.

Here's a newsflash: You are not the prophet Isaiah.

Unless God has audibly given you the command to disturb and distract, then all you are doing is making it more difficult for your congregation to receive you or take you seriously. Inappropriate humor, controversial opinions, unnecessary details, personal confessions, wild accusations, unresolved issues, unrelated information, and confidential information are among the many things that have no place in a sermon. Remember, the goal of the sermon is to spotlight Jesus. If they leave mentioning your addiction but don't mention Jesus, as a preacher you have failed. If the congregation leaves knowing who to vote for but not knowing more about who died for them, you have failed. If the congregation leaves with great information about your subject of choice, but have not grown closer to Jesus, you have failed. Jesus should be at the center of every presentation. The sermon and the preaching moment are not about the preacher; they are about the Savior. The goal of the sermon is always to point others to Jesus.

So how do we get, and make those around us comfortable? Here are a few suggestions:

1. **Command.** *No matter how you preach the sermon, having command of a simple sermon outline that you are able to vocalize from beginning to end will go a long way towards making everyone comfortable.*
2. **Organize.** *Use various rhetorical devices to help you and your congregation internalize the sermon.*
3. **Memorize the points.** *Internalize the introduction, conclusion and illustrations. The more you know, the less inclined you are to fumble when*

the pressure is on.

4. **Flow.** *The sermon should flow conversationally. Writing a manuscript helps the preacher clarify thoughts and solidify transitions to avoid uncomfortable pauses and searching for or misusing words.*
5. **Organic.** *The preacher should never sound like he or she is reading or searching. Neither should the preacher sound canned or stiff. Any expert should be able to talk about their subject with ease, and the microphone in your hand makes you the expert for the moment. The language should be relatable. The illustrations should be believable. Your voice and energy should be recognizable. You are not "playing preacher". Everything about the sermon should be organic.*
6. **Rehearsal.** *The pulpit should not be the first time you preach the sermon. As a matter of fact, the sermon should have been rehearsed both quietly and out loud before it is ever delivered. Time on the treadmill, the morning or evening commute, and the line at the grocery store are all great places to rehearse the sermon. It is also a great idea to talk the sermon over with a friend, as this is also a form of rehearsal. Often, inconsistencies and inaccuracies will present themselves during the rehearsal. If you discover them or a friend points them out, don't be discouraged. Accept constructive criticism and continue to make adjustments. Whatever you do, don't preach the first draft!*
7. **Trust God.** *You have prepared and you have prayed. You have received the message, now it's time to preach. There's no need for hesitation and no cause for fear. The God who called you will be the One who enables you. You have received His message, now go in His power knowing that, "If God be for us, who can be against us."*

We have the sacred privilege of co-laboring with God and we dare not take it lightly. However, just because it is serious doesn't mean it has to be hard. On the contrary, it is because this is so serious that we want to Preach E.A.S.Y. It is precisely because of the important nature of the task at hand that you desire to use every tool at your disposal to effectively, authentically share your story. I pray that this resource will be one of the tools that helps. Whoever you are, wherever you find yourself preaching, I want you to remember always that the God who called you to this assignment will not leave you to do it alone. He will empower you. He has equipped you. He will go with you. And when you have finished and Christ is lifted and God's people are encouraged and inspired, you will discover what so many before you have come to know: God did all the real work all along! I simply did my part.

This was E.A.S.Y. all along.

SELECTED BIBLIOGRAPHY

Anderson, Chris. *TED Talks: The Official TED Guide to Public Speaking.* Boston: Houghton Mifflin Harcourt, 2016.

Davis, H. Grady. *Design For Preaching.* Philadelphia: Fortress Press, 1958.

Dean, Greg. *Step By Step Guide To Stand-Up Comedy.* New Hampshire, Heinemann, 2000.

Galli, Mark., and Craig Brian Larson. *Preaching That Connects: Using The Techniques of Journalists to Add Impact to Your Sermons.* Michigan, Zondervan, 1994

Gallo, Carmine. *Talk Like TED: The 9 Public-Speaking Secrets of the World's Top Minds.* New York, St. Martin's Griffin Books, 2014.

LaRue, Cleophus J. *Power In The Pulpit: How America's Most Effective Black Preachers Prepare Their Sermons.* Louisville, Westminster-John Knox Press, 2002.

Lowry, Eugene L. *The Homiletical Plot: The Sermon As Narrative Art Form.* Atlanta, John Knox Press, 1980

McClure, John S. *Best Advice For Preaching.* Minneapolis, Fortress Press, 1998.

May, Matthew E. *The Laws of Subtraction.* New York, McGraw Hill, 2013

Robinson, Haddon. *Biblical Preaching: The Development and Delivery of Expository Messages.* Michigan, Baker Book House, 1980.

Simmons, Annette. *The Story Factor: Inspiration, Influence and Persuasion Through the Art of Storytelling.* New York: Basic Books, 2001

Thomas, Frank A. *They Like To Never Quit Praising God: The Role of Celebration in Preaching.* Ohio, United Church Press, 1997.

Turpie, Bill. *Ten Great Preacher: Messages and Interviews.* Michigan, Baker Books, 2000.

ADDITIONAL RESOURCES

I've come across a lot of tools that have helped me effectively tell all kinds of stories, especially the story of Jesus. As the song says," these are a few of my favorite things…"

On The Fundamentals Of Preaching
Biblical Preaching by Haddon Robinson
Preaching by Fred Craddock
Design for Preaching by H. Grady Davis

Effective Storytelling
Did I Ever Tell You About The Time? by Grady Jim Robinson
The Story Factor by Annette Simmons
Squirrel Inc. by Stephen Denning

Speaking That Connects
So, You've Been Asked to Speak by Marvin Hunt
The Art of Talking So That People Will Listen by Paul W. Swets
Creative Preaching and Oral Writing by Richard Carl Hoefler

Speaking Without Notes
Speak Without Fear and Without Notes by John Russell Qualley
Speak Up with Confidence by Jack Valenti
Step by Step to Stand-Up Comedy by Greg Dean

Celebration In Preaching
Black Preaching by Henry Mitchell
Celebration & Experience in Preaching by Henry Mitchell
They Like to Never Quit Praising God by Frank Thomas

Sermon Construction
Communicating for a Change by Andy Stanley
Doing the Deed by Martha Simmons
The Homiletic Plot by Joseph Lowery

Narrative Preaching (Examples)
Haddon Robinson: https://youtu.be/2eMoVdmwWZg
Joel Gregory: https://youtu.be/lPdlTdgIn0g
Walter Pearson: https://youtu.be/2xlGoMV_FTw

Celebrative Preaching (Examples)
John Adolph: https://youtu.be/kCsN7HOyS2o
Marcus Cosby: https://youtu.be/sSlNxDP85AM
William Curtis: https://youtu.be/dl2FOfuGpcA

Great Speeches
Robert Kennedy: https://youtu.be/bz7AZxrA16k?list=PL30RAv-0lkxGH_PzKXxU2K-A7dyDOvJIp
Martin Luther King: https://youtu.be/l47Y6VHc3Ms?list=PL30RAv-0lkxGH_PzKXxU2K-A7dyDOvJIp
Barack Obama: https://youtu.be/OFPwDe22CoY

Bibles
New King James Version
New American Standard Version
Message Bible

Commentaries
The Anchor Bible by William Albright and David Freedman
International Critical Commentary by Alfred Plummer
Word Biblical Commentary by F.F. Bruce

Background Resources
IVP Bible Background Commentary: Craig Keener and John Walton
Manners and Customs of the Bible by James M. Freeman
The Desire of Ages by Ellen White

PREACH E.A.S.Y. WORKSHEET

Gamal T. Alexander

Fill in the blanks throughout the worksheet. The resulting answers will help organize your sermon.

Title: _____
Text: _____
Theme: (15 words or less) _____
_____

Introduction:

Connect through a story:

Connect to their story:

Connect to the Bible story:

State the central theme/Ask the central question:

Conversation:

Here's where we provide answers to the central question posted as our core. Our conversation uses exposition (say it), illustrations (show it), and applications (make it stick) to provide answers to the central question.

Point 1	Point 2	Point 3
Explain:	Explain:	Explain:
Illustrate:	Illustrate:	Illustrate:
Apply:	Apply:	Apply:

Climax:

This is what I'm leaving you with: (My most important and impactful idea. Save the best for last!)

This is why it's great! (How will I invite others to join me in celebrating the gospel?) (Is there anybody here?)

This is what I want you to do: (The appeal/call to action)

By this point in the preparation process, the preacher should have developed an outline, written a full manuscript, reviewed the manuscript and created a second outline (based off of the manuscript) inclusive of the revisions that were made. The finish line is in sight! All that's left for the preacher, is to run a final check on the sermon. Prior to rehearsing, use this checklist to determine if the sermon is, in fact, ready to be preached.

Review the outline and answer the following:

1. Is it cohesive?
2. Is it clear?
3. Is my approach creative?
4. Is it concise?
5. Is it contextual?
6. Does it connect?

Further examination is needed to determine whether each section of your outline is ready for the pulpit. The Preach E.A.S.Y. process recognized the sermon as divided into four major categories: Introduction, Applications, Illustrations, and Conclusion. Here are some questions to ask of each category before preaching:

1. Introduction
2. Am I grabbing their attention?
3. Am I developing my argument?
4. Will my congregation be able to follow me?
5. Am I making a clear transition?
6. Applications
7. Do these points come from the text? (Where?)
8. Is this the gospel?
9. Has each point gone as "deep" as I can go?
10. Are these points helpful?
11. Illustrations
12. Do these make the point any clearer?
13. Can these illustrations be any shorter?
14. Are these illustrations appropriate?
15. Are these illustrations believable?
16. Conclusion

17. Have I pointed people to Jesus?
18. Am I ending this sermon on a positive note?
19. Do I have a way to drive my final point home?
20. Am I avoiding introducing new information?
21. Now that you have reviewed the sermon, ask yourself the following:
22. Have I rehearsed the sermon?
23. Have I familiarized myself with/internalized the sermon?
24. Have I spent time in prayer?

ABOUT THE AUTHOR

Gamal Alexander is a passionate storyteller whose mission is to help others to communicate more effectively while himself telling the story of Jesus' love. Born in Brooklyn, NY and raised in Raleigh, NC, he now lives in Southern California where he pastors the Compton Community Church. He coaches, speaks, and writes regularly while traveling across the country. He is the father of two daughters, Faith and Grace. You can find out more about Gamal by visiting www.gamalalexander.com.

www.ingramcontent.com/pod-product-compliance
Lightning Source LLC
Chambersburg PA
CBHW052103110526
44591CB00013B/2327